PREVENTING LEGAL MALPRACTICE

By
JEFFREY M. SMITH
Trotter, Bondurant, Miller & Hishon, Atlanta, Georgia

ST. PAUL, MINN.
WEST PUBLISHING CO.
1981

COPYRIGHT © 1981 By WEST PUBLISHING CO.

All rights reserved

Printed in the United States of America

Library of Congress Cataloging in Publication Data

Smith, Jeffrey M   1947–
    Preventing legal malpractice.

    Includes index.
    1. Lawyers—Malpractice—United States.   I.   Title.
KF313.S55   346.7303'3   80-26759

ISBN 0-8299-2118-4

    Smith Legal Malpractice Pamph.

Dedicated

to

Marcia R. Smith

and

Brandon Michael Smith

Both of whom I missed while completing this work.

PREFACE

Professionals have probably discussed preventing errors and omissions since the first malpractice suit was filed. However, while attorneys undoubtedly participated in those discussions, little was done on an organized basis to prevent legal malpractice until the last few years.

Especially during the last five years, there has been an increased amount of attention and activity in the area of preventing legal malpractice. However, while seminars have included this topic with increasing frequency, relatively few seminars have been given which focused exclusively on preventing legal malpractice. Most of these seminars have been given during the last few years, and available materials have been relatively sketchy.

In 1977, Ronald E. Mallen and I formulated an approach to the area of preventing legal malpractice which we labeled the trichotomy of prevention. It consists of preventing legal malpractice (as well as the incorrect perception by a client that legal malpractice occurred), preventing legal malpractice claims and preventing legal malpractice litigation. This trichotomy of prevention was the basis upon which we proceeded to formulate Chapter Two, Preventing Malpractice, of *Legal Malpractice,* the leading text on the law of legal malpractice, which was authored by Ron Mallen and his partner, Victor B. Levit. Since then, through feedback from numerous seminars in almost half the states, I have attempted to refine and expand on some of the principles which Ron and I discussed in Chapter Two of *Legal Malpractice.*

In analyzing the area of preventing legal malpractice, a number of competing considerations were weighed in determining the content of this work. First, a decision was made to reach as many attorneys as possible. This meant that the size had to be restricted, not only because of price considerations but because of the desire that this work actually be read and utilized by as many attorneys as possible.

Second, the specific topics covered had to be carefully selected and condensed in order to fit within the parameters of the first decision. Chapter One contains the basic trichotomy of prevention, with a relative concentration on the initial client contact, including engagement letters, non-engagement letters and legal fees. Chapter Two focuses on work control, which consists of conflict of interests systems and calendar systems. As is discussed in that Chapter, the term "docket control" has been intentionally discarded because of its narrow focus. The separate chapter on work control reflects the importance, at least on a frequency basis, of preventing errors in the administrative handling of both litigation and non-litigation matters.

Chapter Three is an outgrowth of a prior article I authored for the *South Carolina Law Review*. It represents the first comprehensive written approach to preventing errors in securities transactions, although it hopefully will be followed by a further expansion by Bill Jacobs and me as well as by other authors. While the frequency of claims against attorneys in this area is not that high, the severity of claims, including defense costs, makes this area one of the most critical with respect to prevention techniques. It therefore has received substantial space in this work.

At its quantitative zenith, this work consisted of almost 500 pages in text. Condensing it to its present form has illustrated to me the significance of the adage that: "I am sorry that I did not have time to write a short letter."

In condensing this material, decisions were made to completely excise some material, and reduce the scope of other material. While such decisions can be analyzed to a point which would preclude publishing anything, the topics included and their scope will hopefully be of value to a wide spectrum of attorneys and their support staff, and also be both brief enough and economical enough to gain wide distribution.

Because many of the topics, and several of the approaches used in discussing them, have been derived from comments made by attorneys who attended various seminars, it is only appropriate to request that attorneys who have the opportunity to read this text and who have comments, especially critical ones, be invited to share their views with me. I can assure those who have the time to share those views that they will be carefully considered. If experience is any predictor, a substantial number of those views will be incorporated into the next edition of this work.

JEFFREY M. SMITH

Atlanta, Georgia
December, 1980

SUMMARY OF CONTENTS

CHAPTER 1. PREVENTING LEGAL MALPRACTICE, MALPRACTICE CLAIMS AND MALPRACTICE LITIGATION

CHAPTER 2. WORK CONTROL

CHAPTER 3. PREVENTING ERRORS IN SECURITIES TRANSACTIONS

*

TABLE OF CONTENTS

TABLE OF CONTENTS

TABLE OF CONTENTS

*

TABLE OF CASES

Principal cases are in Italic type. Cases cited in editors' text or notes
are in Roman type. References are to Pages.

TABLE OF CASES

PREVENTING LEGAL MALPRACTICE

Chapter 1

PREVENTING LEGAL MALPRACTICE, MALPRACTICE CLAIMS AND MALPRACTICE LITIGATION *

Jeffrey M. Smith

Section I

PREVENTING LEGAL MALPRACTICE

A. Introduction

Many factors which contribute to client dissatisfaction with the services rendered by their attorneys can be reduced or eliminated through proper office procedures, improved professional relations, and by legal specialization and continuing legal education. At the same time, there are other factors over which attorneys have essentially no control.

In a recent poll,[1] only 25 percent of those interviewed rated the honesty and ethical integrity of attorneys as high. If this is an accurate reflection of the attitude of the population in the United States, then the effort to prevent client dissatisfaction is an uphill struggle.

Attorneys face an additional barrier because many Americans believe those in need of legal services receive only as much justice as they can afford. Even if this idea has been stated so frequently that it is a cliche, unfortunately, there is also a measure of truth in it. Largely due to the availability and utilization of group and private insurance, quality medi-

---

* This Chapter is adapted from material developed by Mr. Smith and Mr. Ronald E. Mallen, previously published in Chapter 2 of Mallen & Levit, LEGAL MALPRACTICE (West Publishing Co. 1977) (hereinafter "Mallen & Levit"). That treatise is recommended for those interested in a comprehensive treatment of the cases and statutes dealing with legal malpractice litigation.

1. Gallup Poll, published August 22, 1976. *See also,* Mendicino v. Magagna, 572 P.2d 21 (Wyo. 1977); Voorhees, *The Ethical Problems of Law Firms,* 24 Prac. Law. 45 (1978); Abramson, *Attorneys, Clients, "Ethics,"* 52 Notre Dame Law. 797 (1977).

1

cal services are available to a greater percentage of people than are quality legal services. Those sources of discontent are magnified both by the age of egalitarianism in which we live and the publicity which is given to the new demands made on attorneys by both clients and governmental agencies.[2]

Finally, some degree of antagonism exists because of the historical reluctance of attorneys to sue other attorneys and testify against their colleagues. This "conspiracy of silence"[3] is not as formidable an obstacle as it once may have been, but some localities, and even some states, remain hostile environments for legal malpractice actions.

There is no panacea for preventing malpractice or for preventing malpractice claims. Even skilled and knowledgeable attorneys make errors in representing their clients. On the other hand, competent representation is, of course, the best defense to a malpractice action.

We cannot escape some types of malpractice claims. There will always be adversaries who seek revenge through malicious use of or abuse of process actions. However, within our control are several primary causes of malpractice claims which arise not because attorneys have been negligent in their representation, but because they have been either derelict in their professional relationship with their clients, or have ineptly managed the business aspects of the practice of law.

It cannot be overemphasized that a good client relationship may not only help in preventing unmeritorious claims but may also be the decisive factor which causes a client to refrain from pursuing a valid claim. The following sections offer suggestions which can assist attorneys in rendering quality legal services, minimize exposure to malpractice claims and improve the attorney-client relationship.

B. Office Procedures

1. *Engagement Letters and Fee Agreements*

As soon as feasible after an attorney is retained, it is both ethically desirable and prudent for an attorney to reach a clear agreement with the client as to the basis of the fee to be charged.[4] The terms of the agreement should be set forth in writing, whether or not the document is referred to as an engagement letter.

However, it is more prudent to do so *prior* to entering into an attorney-client relationship. In addition, the attorney should confirm in writing the timing of fee payments, the scope of the representation, as well as the resolution of any problems which were considered during the initial discussion. In fact, the attorney should consider explaining to the client that an agreement covering these points is a condition precedent to entering into the attorney-client relationship.

2. *E.g., The Troubled Professions, Business Week,* August 16, 1976, at 126.

3. *See* Comment, *Improving Information on Legal Malpractice,* 82 Yale L.J. 590 (1972).

4. ABA Code of Professional Responsibility, EC 2–19. Ethical considerations are aspirational while disciplinary rules are mandatory.

There are several reasons for adopting this approach. First, everyone engages in some degree of rationalization when situations become difficult. In addition, selective recollection is not limited to persons who intend to be difficult clients. If the client focuses initially on the basis of the fee and the other aspects of the representation set forth in the engagement letter, there is less chance that a disagreement will arise in the future. If these matters are not discussed, or are discussed over a period of time, the representation may become a problem waiting to be discovered.

Second, prior to entering into the attorney-client relationship, an attorney is relatively free to negotiate with the client regarding the fee.[5] However, if the fee agreement is unconscionable, courts will of course set it aside.[6] But once the attorney-client relationship exists, all subsequent fee agreements are subject to the presumption of voidability which affects fiduciaries, including attorneys.[7] A fee agreement which is altered late in the course of a representation will be subject to even closer scrutiny.[8]

Third, from a practical point of view, the best time to negotiate a fee is when the client seeks the attorney's services. At that time, a client is concerned about the legal problem and the ability of the attorney to assist in its solution. After the problem is resolved or proves to be insoluble, the attorney's value, in the client's perception, will usually decline.

The form of the engagement letter is far less important than its existence.[9] It can be a formal letter, a contract with signature lines for the attorney and client, or an informal letter which simply confirms the details of a previous discussion. If the latter format is utilized, consideration should be given to asking the client to acknowledge receipt of the letter by an independent written confirmation in order to avoid subsequent disagreements.

Because it is difficult to predict in advance the representations which will involve a dispute, attorneys should consider whether to include a provision covering withdrawal prior to undertaking a particular matter. This is especially important in securities transactions. This should include the disposition of any funds previously paid as a retainer. Withdrawal provisions are subject to ethical scrutiny[10] as well as to the rules of practice of various courts and administrative agencies. However, these provisions and rules permit flexibility, and an understanding can be reached which may prevent an attorney from being sued for breach of contract or withdrawing improperly.

5. Elmore v. Johnson, 143 Ill. 513, 32 N.E. 413 (1892).

6. McCreary v. Joel, 186 So.2d 4 (Fla. 1966).

7. Randolph v. Schuyler, 284 N.C. 496, 201 S.E.2d 833 (1974); Rader v. Thrasher, 57 Cal.2d 244, 18 Cal.Rptr. 736, 368 P.2d 360 (1962).

8. Kravis v. Smith Marine, Inc., 60 Ill.2d 141, 324 N.E.2d 417 (1975); Berman v. Coakley, 257 Mass. 159, 153 N.E. 463 (1926).

9. Steele & Nimmer, *Lawyers, Clients, and Professional Regulation,* 1976 A.B.F. Res. J., 919, 1008.

10. *E.g.,* ABA Code of Professional Responsibility, DR 2–110, ECs 2–31 and 2–32.

2. *Non-Engagement Letters*

An increasing concern for attorneys is the possibility of a non-client asserting that the attorney owed and breached a duty giving rising to both standing and a valid cause of action. Among other areas, this problem encompasses claims by opposing parties in litigation, will beneficiaries and investors. The cases and literature in this area continue to expand.[11]

Suits by opposing parties for malicious use or abuse of process are not open to treatment by non-engagement letters. Such actions are based on allegedly malicious conduct and, if true, such conduct cannot be defended based upon the contents of a non-engagement letter.

Similarly, various statutes, including the Securities Act of 1933 and the Securities Exchange Act of 1934, impose duties which cannot be bargained away. In addition, certain implied causes of action which have been recognized by courts under the federal securities acts cannot be defended based upon non-engagement letters.

However, many actions which have been brought against attorneys could have been defended with comparative ease if non-engagement letters had been utilized. In general, such letters should be considered when the representation involves contact with parties other than the client who retained the attorney who may reasonably rely on the work product or advice of the attorney.

The contents of the non-engagement letter will vary of course depending on the type of representation and the particular facts. A typical example is a real estate transaction where the attorney in question represents a lender and neither the seller nor purchaser are represented. Although the fees of such an attorney are usually paid by the purchaser who obtained the loan, most lenders and attorneys representing lenders do not look at the purchaser as a client of the lender's attorney. However, because the overall atmosphere is conducive to such a purchaser in fact relying on the lender's attorney, use of a non-engagement letter should be considered.

In this situation, the letter should clearly state that the attorney is representing only the lender and is not analyzing the transaction for the benefit of the purchaser. To the extent that there are any exceptions, they should be separately listed and identified as such. There should be a specific recommendation that the purchaser retain an independent attorney.

When an attorney is requested to prepare a will or trust, a different problem is presented. In a real estate transaction, the lender will not object, and might insist if properly apprised, to the use of a non-engagement letter; however, a donor of a trust may well object to a disclaimer of any duty to beneficiaries. In fact, it might cause a client to seek

---

11. *See* citations in Chapter 4, Mallen & Levit, LEGAL MALPRACTICE, (West Publishing Co. 1977).

another attorney to draft a will or trust. Nonetheless, in certain instances, the possibility of relatives disagreeing over the interpretation of a will or trust should be raised to the client. This may present a practical opportunity to suggest including in the engagement letter with the client an express provision that the client agrees the legal work is only for his or her benefit and not for the benefit of those named in the document. Particularly in those cases where various relatives are aware of the details of the will or trust, actual non-engagement letters could prove useful.

It should also be noted that non-clients have asserted standing even when previously represented by independent counsel. Such letters should therefore be considered in all instances where it appears other attorneys may not be called upon or may not undertake to provide the full scope of legal services called for by a particular transaction.

Non-engagement letters can also be utilized in situations where representation is either declined or where the attorney withdraws. In either instance, there may be a question regarding the existence of the attorney-client relationship at one or more points in time, and questions may also arise regarding the duty of an attorney even if there is never an actual undertaking to perform services for the "client." Non-engagement letters of this type should normally include warnings regarding potential statute of limitations problems. In addition, it is useful to include a suggestion that the prospective or former client consider seeking a second opinion. The failure to utilize this type of non-engagement letter can easily lead to a malpractice suit.[12]

3. *Legal Fees*

There are three primary ways in which legal fees contribute to malpractice claims. First, client dissatisfaction with fees, even if paid, may be the catalyst in the future for a malpractice suit. Second, fees which are paid under protest as being excessive can lead to legal action to recover the excess, and may also involve direct claims of legal malpractice. Finally, as discussed more fully below, suits initiated by attorneys to collect fees are, with increasing frequency, engendering counterclaims alleging legal malpractice.[13] Many of these problems can be prevented by reaching an early agreement regarding legal fees.

The ABA Code of Professional Responsibility mandates that "[a] lawyer shall not enter into an agreement for, charge, or collect an illegal or clearly excessive fee."[14] Demonstrating the need for revision, it suggests that an excessive fee can be charged, as long as it is not "clearly excessive."

---

12. Togstad v. Vesely, Otto, Miller & Keefe, 291 N.W.2d 686 (Minn. 1980). *See* Chapter 3, Section V, *infra*.

13. *E.g.*, Felger v. Nichols, 35 Md.App. 182, 370 A.2d 141 (1977); Nickerson v. Martin, 34 Conn.Sup. 22, 374 A.2d 258 (1976); Kravis v. Smith Marine, Inc., 60 Ill.2d 141, 324 N.E.2d 417 (1975).

14. ABA Code of Professional Responsibility, DR 2–106(A).

Disciplinary Rule 2–106(B), however, states that "[a] fee is clearly excessive . . . [if it] is in excess of a reasonable fee." In determining the reasonableness of a fee, eight factors are enumerated:

(1) The time and labor required, the novelty and difficulty of the questions involved, and the skill requisite to perform the legal service properly.

(2) The likelihood, if apparent to the client, that the acceptance of the particular employment will preclude other employment by the lawyer.

(3) The fee customarily charged in the locality for similar legal services.

(4) The amount involved and the results obtained.

(5) The time limitations imposed by the client or by the circumstances.

(6) The nature and length of the professional relationship with the client.

(7) The experience, reputation, and ability of the lawyer or lawyers performing the services.

(8) Whether the fee is fixed or contingent.

While the setting of fees is not a science, it can and should be an organized art. If factors such as those contained in the Code are utilized and if the analysis is reflected in writing, a complaint by a dissatisfied client as to the propriety of the fee will be more easily explained. Likewise, a suit to collect legal fees will be more likely to succeed.

Many attorneys use a standard hourly fee for all of their work. While this has many administrative advantages, it has a potential drawback. If a fee is questioned, a point of attack may be the uniformity of the hourly rate. A possible inference to be drawn from such uniformity is that the rate was set without regard to the factors set forth in Disciplinary Rule 2–106(B); it is certainly unlikely that analyzing the eight factors could lead to a uniform hourly rate. Thus, ethical considerations and disciplinary rules can become indirect standards in civil litigation even if they cannot be sued upon directly.[15]

The use of retainers can also contribute to malpractice claims. Problems usually do not arise with respect to retainers for general representation, because the attorney or law firm has agreed to perform either unlimited or specified services in exchange for an agreed-upon amount. The difficulties usually concern retainers which are required as an advance for a particular case. Monthly or other periodic fee statements are charged against the retainer, usually with an agreement that an additional retainer may be required. Accurate record keeping is essential to avoid disputes. The engagement letter should cover the disposition of any remaining funds if the matter terminates or the attorney withdraws prior to the expenditure of the entire retainer.

15. *I.e.,* Matter of Charles Willie L., 63 Cal.App.3d 760, 132 Cal.Rptr. 840 (1976). *See* Wolfram, *The Code of Professional Responsibility as a Measure of Attorney Liability in Civil Litigation,* 30 S.Car.L.Rev. 281 (1979).

The type of account in which a retainer is placed is also important. In the absence of compelling reasons, substantial funds should be placed in interest-bearing accounts which have withdrawal privileges corresponding to the intervals between fee statements. Crediting this interest to clients may not produce a significant aggregate amount, but it will demonstrate attentiveness to cost control as well as awareness of fiduciary obligations. This may reduce or eliminate concern by the client over the total amount of the fee and may also contribute to rapport which prevents other problems from arising.

Billing procedures are integrally related to timekeeping and all other aspects of legal fees. Even if the so-called "one line" fee statement is used, it is important to record the time spent and the activities undertaken in particular matters. If the basis of the fee is questioned, time records can be critical in preventing a claim and determining the outcome if one is made.

The frequency and format of billing vary not only from attorney to attorney, but from matter to matter. However, as a general rule fee statements should be itemized or, at a minimum, state that an itemization will be forwarded upon request. As one does not know in advance which cases may be subject to a dispute, or which case may ultimately be resolved by a jury, it is important to have a system that provides a comprehensive and relatively clear record.

The frequency of billing is possibly more important than the format.[16] Even if the format is objectionable to the client, or if the total fee is questioned, the problem will often be minor if the client is billed on a monthly basis. Statements for fees and expenses are more palatable when billed on a frequent interim basis rather than as a relatively large charge. By the end of the case, or even the end of six months, the potential problem may have increased substantially. Not only will the total amount of money in controversy be higher, but the opportunity to resolve the problem by incremental billing will have been lost. Even in instances where the fee is to be paid annually or at the end of a matter, it may be helpful to forward fee statements on an interim basis, stating in a cover letter that it is for informational purposes only.

Approximately 20 to 30 percent of all legal malpractice litigation is caused, directly or indirectly, by dissatisfaction with or actual disputes over legal fees. This should not be surprising since a large majority of legal representations involve monetary issues. The chances are excellent that if a firm sues to collect legal fees, payment will not be made by the client and a counterclaim will be brought for legal malpractice. It thus becomes important to consider carefully the possible risks attendant to a suit for legal fees prior to commencing such an action.

16. *E.g., see* Neville v. Davinroy, 41 Ill. App.3d 706, 355 N.E.2d 86 (1976). In this action to recover legal fees, the court expressly noted that the failure of the attorney to provide timely bills could have misled his client and deprived him of an opportunity to appreciate the time and effort expended on his behalf.

Unlike many of our predecessors in England, most practicing attorneys are dependent upon reasonably prompt payment by clients in order to continue practicing. When clients do not pay promptly, most attorneys are prudent enough to make reasonable inquiry. Nonetheless, in all too many instances attorneys finally threaten or institute a legal action to collect the fees. Such action generally carries with it more potential risk than reward given the reality that clients who do not pay generally do not have the ability to pay or do not feel it is appropriate to pay. Especially in the latter instance, a counterclaim is to be expected.

The client may have funds available but may have also determined that there are other pressing priorities which are more important than payment of legal fees. In addition, the client may believe that the statement is too high without regard to the results achieved, or may believe that the fees would have been appropriate had the desired results been achieved.

If a client is simply unable to pay, a firm may press forward and obtain a judgment, but will have expended additional time and expense with no tangible result, unless it is willing to proceed with garnishments, levying or a bankruptcy proceeding. These are generally not desirable courses of action because of the public relations impact. In addition, a person who currently is unable to pay, and is consequently not the most desirable client, may later become economically successful. One way to ensure that such a client returns for legal services in the future is to treat the client in a manner which generates feelings of loyalty as opposed to resentment.

In those instances where a firm has analyzed the matter and believes a suit for legal fees and expenses should be filed, it is important to first review Ethical Consideration 2–23 of the Code of Professional Responsibility:

> A lawyer should be zealous in his efforts to avoid controversies over fees with clients and should attempt to resolve amicably any differences on the subject. He should not sue a client for a fee unless necessary to prevent fraud or gross imposition by the client.

Clients rarely commit fraud in failing to pay a statement for fees and expenses and, if this Ethical Consideration is followed, the analysis generally will be limited to whether a "gross imposition" has occurred. Ethical Considerations are generally aspirational in nature. However, the failure to follow this particular Ethical Consideration may lead to problem-ridden litigation, as well as an unsuccessful suit, especially if the client's new attorney succeeds in introducing into evidence the failure to adhere to this Ethical Consideration.

Assuming that a firm has determined that a gross imposition has occurred, there are several other significant areas which must be analyzed before instituting a suit. First, consideration must be given to the factors in Disciplinary Rule 2–106(B) which include the time, labor, customary fee, amount involved, results obtained and experience of the attorney.

If, after a review of these factors, a firm is not convinced that the fee in question is reasonable, then the fee should be voluntarily reduced and a request made that the reduced fee be paid. Moreover, if a firm is convinced that the fee either is not reasonable or is subject to serious question, it may be more appropriate to request the client to indicate what is perceived to be a reasonable fee.

Second, at this point in the analysis of a potential claim against a client, it is beneficial to consult an attorney who has not been directly involved in the representation. Certainly it is possible that a member of the same firm could be objective, but an attorney from another firm is potentially a better choice. This is certainly true if the fee in question is significant and if there is a perception that the client is litigious.

Among other reasons for securing an independent attorney, there is a risk that the suit to collect fees may involve a violation of Canon 4 of the Code of Professional Responsibility, which proscribes revealing either confidences or secrets of a client. The only exception in this area is Disciplinary Rule 4–101(C)(4) which states an attorney may reveal:

> Confidences or secrets *necessary* to establish or collect his fee or to defend himself or his employees or associates against an accusation of wrongful conduct.

Clearly, wholesale disclosure of a client's secrets and confidences is not "necessary." Without an objective independent attorney, there is an increased danger that unnecessary disclosure will occur.

Third, the firm must analyze the actual, as opposed to theoretical, recovery which might be achieved. In general, the potential recovery from the client is *never* the actual amount of the statement for fees and expenses, even if a firm is convinced that the total fees and expenses are reasonable. The following factors all reduce the potential recovery, even though some of these factors are fairly subjective:

(1) The cost of retaining an independent attorney to represent the firm (the assumption being that no one wants a fool for a client);

(2) The time expended by members of the firm in working with the new attorney to answer interrogatories, prepare for depositions and plan for trial;

(3) The portion of the projected recovery which will be paid in income taxes;

(4) The overall risk of a counterclaim, including the risk that it will be asserted, the chances of an adverse judgment, the range of the potential judgment and the possibility it will not be covered by professional liability insurance;

(5) The fact that the client might have been a desirable client in the future, but certainly will not be once litigation is instituted; and

(6) The adverse public relations impact, over and above the impact of the former client's direct criticism.

Assume that a particular statement for fees and expenses totals $12,-000.00 and that, after evaluation, a firm determines that it is reasonable. If an independent attorney is retained on a contingent fee, the firm will not recover more than $9,000.00 in most cases. In addition, 25 percent and very possibly a higher percentage may be paid in taxes. Assuming that the average tax bracket of the partners in the firm is 25 percent, the $9,000.00 recovery is reduced to $6,750.00. The more subjective considerations must also be factored into the equation, with the ultimate result that the $12,000.00 statement for fees and expenses is reduced to something less than $5,000.00 depending on the emphasis placed on various subjective factors.

Once this sum is divided among the partners in the particular firm, a serious question should exist with respect to whether instituting a suit is prudent. At a minimum, suits against clients for legal fees and expenses should be an exception, not a rule.

4. *Communication*

The comprehensiveness and frequency of communication is important in and of itself and is also a significant variable with respect to proper billing. In fact, billing should be considered a form of communication which can apprise the client of the services rendered by his attorney.

If the attorney regularly discusses matters in person and by telephone with his client, confirms these discussions and significant events in writing, and forwards pertinent documents on a regular basis, then fee statements can be forwarded on a less frequent basis with less itemization.

Communication is, in many respects, at the center of all legal services. However, it is far more useful for preventing malpractice claims than for preventing malpractice. It is therefore treated more fully in Section II of this Chapter.

5. *File Organization and Maintenance*

Proper file organization is crucial in preventing many of the errors which result in malpractice claims. The first step is the one that is most frequently omitted: bringing to bear on the particular matter the legal talent necessary to determine the full scope of the matter. A file cannot be properly organized unless the attorney in charge of the file is aware of the range of opportunities and problems.

This procedure is usually routine when attorneys are faced with large mergers or complex commercial litigation. However, it also applies to seemingly less sophisticated legal matters. For example, litigation concerning a small limited partnership which acquired one piece of undeveloped real estate may involve questions of law in the areas of real estate, tax, securities, usury, professional responsibility and civil procedure. It is unlikely that any one attorney is qualified to resolve all the problems in these diverse areas, and it is even less likely that any one attorney can determine the existence of all the problems.

Once a matter has been divided into component parts and assignments have been made, attorneys must establish a system for storage of the active file. Attorneys or legal assistants working on a matter may have need to keep a portion of the file at their desk. If so, those portions of the file must be duplicated. In general, the entire file should be available on short notice. This requires central storage of the entire file; at least it must be stored in one place consistently. In addition, when it is removed, a checkout card must be signed and put in place of the file.

Handling documents is another aspect of file organization which must be done properly to prevent malpractice. If a document is unique, it deserves its own section in the file. If, as is generally the case, it is part of the series of related documents, then it belongs in an indexed file system. Not only must the documents be separated by some mechanical means such as numbered tabs, but there must be a written index which identifies the documents and the corresponding index numbers. The use of three and four ring notebooks should always be considered. It is frequently useful to use subject matter tabs across the top of a notebook, from A to Z, and numerical tabs down the side within each subject matter category.

In large transactions, overlapping index systems may be desirable. For example, a large antitrust matter may involve several related cases. Each must have its own index. Certain aspects of the cases, such as document production, may also require a separate index. However, a central index should also be utilized.

After a matter has been concluded, document preservation deserves careful attention. In jurisdictions which apply the occurrence rule to statutes of limitations in legal malpractice actions,[17] document preservation can be theoretically limited to the number of years specified in the statute, starting with the termination of the transaction. However, even in jurisdictions with the occurrence rule, there are situations in which the statute of limitations can be tolled and, therefore, reliance cannot be placed on a fixed period of time.

In those jurisdictions which apply the discovery rule,[18] documents must be preserved for a reasonably long period of time. The attorney engaged in a trusts and estates practice should consider retaining documents for 20 years or more in such jurisdictions.

It cannot be overemphasized that an attorney's file is more likely to be of assistance in defending a legal malpractice action than it will be in supporting the client's claim. Moreover, the destruction of the file soon after a transaction is completed may support an inference that the file contained material which demonstrated the alleged malpractice. A systematic approach to file organization will not only prevent many of the

17. The majority of jurisdictions apply the occurrence rule under which a statute of limitations period commences at the time all essential aspects of the cause of action have occurred, regardless of whether the client discovers the pertinent facts. *See* Chapter 10, Mallen & Levit.

18. *See* Mallen & Levit, Chapter 10.

errors which have been the subject of litigation, but will also preserve what may be the essential evidence to defend a malpractice claim.

6. *Use of Firm Facilities*

The law firm should discourage the personal use of its facilities and stationery by its principals and employees. If it does not, it takes the risk of liability for non-firm-related activity. Although the firm may ultimately be able to establish that it was not involved in the transaction, exculpation may be a lengthy and expensive process.[19]

7. *Work Control*

Systems for determining conflicts of interests and for calendar functions constitute the broad area of "work control." The term "docket control" is not utilized in this text because it does not include the conflicts system and, within the calendar area, is too narrow a term. It generally is viewed as a litigation tool when, in fact, all areas of practice are subject to calendar control.

Work control systems can be a major factor in preventing malpractice. While statistics are not yet reliable in this area, in most jurisdictions, it is likely that between 20 and 50 percent of all malpractice claims involve allegations that a time-related error occurred. However, many such cases never should have been undertaken in the first place. In addition, on close inspection, in many cases the *reason* the client sued was dissatisfaction over fees, or a general lack of rapport.

Nonetheless, work control is a significant area for preventing malpractice. As such, Chapter 2 has been devoted entirely to this subject.

8. *Financial Controls*

With certain exceptions, it is a basic ethical requirement that funds paid to attorneys for the benefit of clients must be identified and properly segregated.[20] This requires that attorneys maintain one or more trust accounts and, when necessary, establish escrow accounts. Except in unusual circumstances, no one other than an attorney should be on a signature card.

Establishing and maintaining proper records with respect to such accounts will not prevent dishonest conduct. However, the maintenance of current cash flow statements, receivable accounts and records reflecting the aging of receivables can provide early warning of a shortage of funds. Problems involving funds held in trust have produced their fair share of malpractice claims.[21] Because of general agency and fiduciary principles, each attorney must not only act properly but also ensure that

---

19. *See, e.g.*, Peterson v. Harville, 445 F.Supp. 16 (D. Or. 1977).

20. ABA Code of Professional Responsibility, EC 9–5 and DR 9–102.

21. *E.g.*, Amsler v. American Home Assur. Co., 348 So.2d 68 (Fla.App. 1977); In re Snitoff, 53 Ill.2d 50, 289 N.E.2d

other members of the firm do so; as a rule, attorneys are liable for the misappropriation of client funds by partners and employees.[22]

C. Professional Relations

1. *Outside the Law Firm*

Other professions, such as the medical profession, routinely match particular knowledge and skills to specific problems. The two ways in which this has been accomplished are to associate specialists or to refer cases outright. The legal profession has not done as well in this area, primarily because it has been slower to develop specialization.

Attorneys undertaking matters which they are not competent to handle are prime candidates to become defendants in malpractice actions. While it is always possible and ethically permissible to become competent after undertaking a matter,[23] this may not be in the best interests of the client or the attorney.

Ethical considerations dictate that an attorney should not undertake a legal matter which he knows or should know is beyond his competence, unless a competent lawyer is associated.[24] While the failure to do so may not be negligence in and of itself, it will certainly provide the basis for a cause of action for negligence if the services rendered are deficient.

Where the firm does not possess the necessary expertise, the matter may be assigned to an attorney who feels compelled to proceed as if he were fully competent to determine the full range of opportunities and problems without any assistance. In litigation, this can easily lead to a failure to raise an affirmative defense or to plead all appropriate causes of action. It can also cause less obvious errors such as failure to obtain the most favorable settlement due to a lack of knowledge of the substantive law. In corporate matters, this situation can lead to improperly secured collateral or noncompliance with securities registration provisions.

However, problems arise even in firms where the necessary expertise does exist. There are numerous attorneys in relatively large firms who desire to practice in several diverse areas of law, generally because of intellectual interest and/or concern over losing control of clients. One of the dangers associated with this is a possible tendency to overlook issues, since other attorneys would have to be consulted if the issues were raised. While this behavior may not be intentional, it is a significant problem for some attorneys.

Although referring the client to another attorney may not be immediately profitable, it may be the only way to prevent malpractice and, in the long run, may prove financially beneficial. If properly explained, the

---

428 (1972), *cert. denied* 412 U.S. 906, 93 S.Ct. 2292 (1973).

22. *E.g.,* Blackmon v. Hale, 1 Cal.3d 548, 83 Cal.Rptr. 194, 463 P.2d 418 (1970).

23. ABA Code of Professional Responsibility, EC 6–4.

24. ABA Code of Professional Responsibility, DR 6–101(A)(1). *But see* Horne v. Peckham, 97 Cal.App.3d 404, 158 Cal.Rptr. 714 (1979).

client will gain confidence in the referring attorney's abilities and integrity. If referral or association of other counsel is desirable, the attorney should be sure that the client gives informed consent, preferably in writing, to the referral or association.

2. *Inside the Law Firm*

Proper interaction between attorneys within a firm can be an important factor in preventing malpractice. A catharsis is unnecessary; but, it can be helpful for attorneys to share with each other the types of errors they have made, the reasons the errors occurred, and the solutions (if any) which were found. This type of interaction is part of what the author views as the "psychology of errors." While there may be an excuse for attorneys making an error for the first time, repetition of the error within the same firm is certainly less excusable.

Another aspect of the "psychology of errors" is systematic reinforcement of attorneys within a firm for spotting potential problems and actual errors. In many firms, especially if raised by an associate, the admission of an error is likely to result in criticism.

Law firms should consider only moderate reinforcement for actually solving problems and errors. This is especially true for younger attorneys. Once an attorney realizes that an error occurred and that there is a potential for a malpractice claim, he may lose objectivity. Unless the attorney obtains assistance, his attempts to solve the problem may magnify it instead.

Another procedure for preventing malpractice which is connected to professional relations within the law firm involves the "bad case review." Malpractice claims occur with surprising frequency in connection with matters which were unattractive from a monetary, emotional and/or intellectual point of view. Very few attorneys are so busy that they fail to file a complaint in a timely manner in a case where the client can either pay the hourly fee or where the contingent fee agreed upon is particularly attractive. Similarly, clients who are in the process of establishing what appears to be a successful business are not the ones who are neglected through improper incorporation. A periodic review by other attorneys in the firm of those matters categorized as "bad cases" may prevent the type of oversights which such cases can produce. In order to ensure that this procedure does not break down, at least three cases should periodically be selected, even if they cannot clearly be labeled as "bad cases." Review of the cases should be on a "buddy" system.

3. *Malpractice Claims Analysis*

Considering the significant increase in the frequency and volume of legal malpractice claims, it is very probable that an attorney will at some point either be the subject of a claim or be consulted by a client seeking assistance in suing another attorney.

If you are consulted regarding a potential claim against another attorney, you should be careful not to criticize the attorney's conduct until you have been fully apprised of all material facts. Less than 50 percent of legal malpractice claims prove successful for the client, either in judgment or settlement. There is a reasonable chance that the client's dissatisfaction with the attorney is attributable to lack of information or a breakdown in the attorney-client relationship. Moreover, even if the attorney erred or was negligent, it is still possible that no attorney could have obtained a better result. Therefore, an attorney consulted about a legal malpractice claim should exercise caution before pursuing litigation.

The attorney-defendant should be careful to maintain his insurance protection, but he should not unnecessarily disclose the fact or extent of his coverage to the adverse claimant. Such disclosure may be the financial encouragement which causes a legal malpractice claim.

The risk of a malpractice claim mandates that the attorney carefully preserve all professional liability insurance policies. Those policies written on an occurrence basis may provide the only insurance available for a claim made in the distant future. Other types of forms, such as the claims made or claims that "may be made," can also provide coverage for claims made in the future. This mainly involves the so-called "risk tail" coverage and extended reporting endorsements. Similarly, the attorney should retain all excess or "umbrella" policies because they form part of the basic insurance protection.[25]

The attorney should not attempt to defend his own malpractice claim. Of course, the fact that a malpractice action is brought does not indicate that the attorney erred or was negligent. Nonetheless, it has been the experience of those who regularly defend legal malpractice actions that the majority of the attorneys who have been negligent do not recognize their errors until explained by an independent attorney. In addition, there are key issues of credibility involved in a disagreement between the attorney and client as to what actually transpired. One cannot be a witness in such litigation and competently represent himself as an advocate for his own credibility.

D. Legal Specialization

In 1953, the American Bar Association formed the Committee on Specialization and Specialized Legal Education. Since that time, the action taken by the ABA has demonstrated that specialization is a subject which interests many attorneys, but to which there is an abundance of opposition.[26] Notwithstanding the lack of progress by the ABA, significant attention has been devoted to specialization.[27] Specialization and

---

25. *See* Chapter 18, Mallen & Levit.

26. *Final Report of the Committee on Specialization of the State Bar of California*, 44 Cal. St. B.J. 493 (1969).

27. *E.g.*, Weber, *Why Formal Legal Specialization?*, 63 A.B.A.J. 951 (1977); Cote, *Self-Designation for Michigan Lawyers, What is it All About?*, 56 Mich. St. B.J. 107 (1977); Fromson, *Let's Be Realistic About Specialization*, 63 A.B.A.J. 74 (1977); *Has the Time Come for National Standards?*, 63 A.B.A.J. 18 (1977); Standing Committee on Specialization, *Interim Reports Discussion Draft*, ABA Report (October 1976); Peterson, *Specialization? Relicensing? What Young Lawyers Think*, Barrister, Fall, 1976 at 26; Bresnahan & Kane, *Professional Ethics and Competence in Trial Practice*, 62 A.B.A.J. 988 (1976); Puffer, *Specialization*, Barrister, Win-

designation programs have been adopted in several states, including Arizona, California, Colorado, Florida, Georgia, North Dakota, New Mexico and Texas.

California adopted the first specialization plan in February of 1971,[28] although the plan was not actually put into effect until 1973. Rules and regulations were officially adopted in 1974.[29] This plan originally encompassed only the fields of criminal law, taxation and workman's compensation, but expansion was planned to include bankruptcy, probate, labor and family law.[30] It is a certification-type plan and certification is based upon a combination of continuing legal education, experience and involvement in the particular specialty and the successful completion of a written examination. Recertification is required every five years. A certified specialist is entitled to advertise in a classified telephone directory.

Arizona,[31] Colorado,[32] and Texas,[33] have adopted programs similar to California's. A variation of the California plan has been adopted in North Dakota but is restricted to the area of trial practice. Similar proposals have been discussed in other jurisdictions.[34]

Florida, Georgia and New Mexico have taken a different approach and have adopted self-designation or advertising plans. In the New Mexico plan in order to be certified as a specialist, a significant percentage of an attorney's time for the past five years must have been devoted to the area being designated. That percentage must remain constant. There are also rules relating to the referral of clients where the referral is based on an attorney's designation. Attorneys may select from over 35 fields of law and, depending on which of two "advertising" options is selected, may designate either one or up to three areas of law.[35]

Florida has taken an intermediate approach which requires substantial experience in the areas designated. Every three years the attorney must again qualify and must have attended at least 30 hours of continuing legal education in each designated area. The attorney can select up to three areas from an extensive list.[36] Recently, Georgia has adopted a designation plan similar to Florida's.

ter, 1976, at 76; Zehnle, *Specialization in the Legal Profession,* 1975 A.B.F. Res. J., selected bibliography at 45; *Legal Specialization and Certification,* 61 Va.L.Rev. 434 (1975); Eiger & Morrison, *Legal Specialization in Illinois; Designation, Certification or Stagnation?,* 63 Ill. B.J. 296 (1975); *Specialization; an Overview,* 69 Cum. L.Rev. 453 (1975); Teschner, *Certification of Legal Specialists: Skeptical Views of a Chicago Country Lawyer,* 62 Ill. B.J. 658 (1974).

28. *See* 46 Cal. St. B.J. 182 (1971).

29. *See* 49 Cal. St. B.J. 170 (1974).

30. *See* 51 Cal. St. B.J. 549, 555 (1976).

31. Arizona, like California, certifies specialists in criminal law, taxation and workman's compensation.

32. The Colorado pilot program provides for certification in tax, securities and labor law.

33. The Texas plan includes criminal law, family law and labor law. *See Legal Specialization Comes to Texas,* 38 Tex. B.J. 235 (1975).

34. Kentucky (tax, labor, patent, trademark, copyright, securities and transportation law); New Jersey; Oregon (several proposals voted down).

35. New Mexico Sup.Ct. Rule 32, *See* 12 N.M. St. B. Bull. 250 (July 5, 1973).

36. Admiralty; appellate practice; antitrust; bankruptcy; corporation and business law; criminal law; estate planning and administration; family

Specialization has been cited as a means of improving competence in the legal profession.[37] Although there are problems with specialization plans,[38] it appears likely that other states will adopt some type of specialization plan and that an increasing number of attorneys will participate.

Specialization as a means of preventing malpractice is premised on the theory that an attorney who specializes will be more competent and less likely to make procedural and substantive errors. But specialization will not prevent all errors. For example, the office procedures set forth above apply equally to all attorneys. Also, specialization will not eliminate time-related errors, except those errors attributable to an attorney's failure to know the statutes of limitations in a specialty area.

Specialization can also complicate malpractice litigation. For example, application of the standard of care will probably be different, and expert testimony will not only be required but the witness must be a specialist.

Specialization also affects the attorney-client relationship. The more the attorney specializes the more likely he is to handle legal matters for clients on a one-time basis. This is certainly true of those clients referred by another attorney. Not only will an attorney who specializes have less opportunity to build good rapport with clients, but the expectations of clients will in many instances have been raised by knowledge of the attorney's specialization. Thus, even though specialization may prevent malpractice concerning procedural and substantive law, it carries with it the potential for problems, which calls for special attention regarding client relations.

E. Continuing Legal Education

Like specialization, continuing legal education has been cited as a method of preventing malpractice by increasing the competence of lawyers in both procedural and substantive law. To the extent that continuing legal education also includes law office management and malpractice prevention programs, it can be even more effective.

Although continuing legal education has been described as an important means of increasing professional competence,[39] opinions are not

law; international law; environmental law; consumer law; labor law; patent, trademark and copyright; real property law; taxation; trial practice; workman's compensation; administration and governmental law; registered general practice; and personal injury and wrongful death.

37. Brink, *Let's Take Specialization Apart,* 62 A.B.A.J. 191 (1976).

38. Approximately 82.5 percent of those certified in California during the first year of operation came in under the grandfather clause. This requires only

that the attorney has been admitted to practice for ten years and has substantial involvement in the field. Zehnle, *Specialization in the Legal Profession,* 1975 Am. B. Foundation Res. J. at 5.

39. *E.g.,* Sheran & Harmon, *Minnesota Plan: Mandatory Continuing Legal Education for Lawyers and Judges as a Condition for Maintaining Professional Licensing,* 44 Fordham L.Rev. 1081 (1976); Wolkin, *A Better Way to Keep Lawyers Competent,* 61 A.B.A.J. 574 (1975).

uniform on the subject.[40] Continuing education, however, is becoming a part of the modern attorney's professional life. Minnesota has adopted a mandatory continuing legal education program for both attorneys and judges [41] which requires 45 hours of legal education over each three-year period. Iowa was the second state to adopt such a program.[42] Since then, similar programs have been adopted by other states.[43]

Continuing legal education is certainly here to stay, and will continue to expand both as an educational opportunity and as a requirement for maintaining a license to practice law.[44] Nevertheless, as a means of preventing malpractice, it is only as effective as the effort which is devoted to it.[45]

Section II

PREVENTING LEGAL MALPRACTICE CLAIMS

A. Client Relations

1. *Interpersonal Relations*

Notwithstanding the litigiousness of our society, civil actions are not filed for every error or for every negligent act. Although the rapport developed between attorneys and clients will not prevent malpractice, it can assist in preventing malpractice claims.[46]

The most common complaint by clients is that their attorneys failed to give the matter sufficient attention and that this lack of diligence caused the case to be lost.[47] The impression of the "neglectful" attorney, which

40. Wolkin, *A Better Way to Keep Law-yers Competent,* 61 A.B.A.J. 574 (1975).

41. Sheran & Harmon, *Minnesota Plan, supra,* note 40.

42. *Id.*

43. Wisconsin and Washington. *See, Mandatory CLE Comes To Washington,* ALI–ABA CLE Review, April 8, 1977, at 1.

44. *E.g.,* Unterberger, *Lawyer's 1976 View of Continuing Legal Education,* 22 Prac. Law. 71 (1976); Byron, *Mandatory Continuing Education in Minnesota: The First Year,* 50 St. Johns L.Rev. 512 (1976); Hardy, *Continuing Legal Education in Kentucky: A Mandatory Plan,* 40 Ky. Bench & B. 10 (1976); Sheran & Harmon, *Minnnesota Plan, supra,* note 39; Byron, *Mandatory Continuing Legal Education in Minnesota,* 54 Mich. St. B.J. 361 (1975); Leete & Loeb, *Continuing Legal Education— Should It Be Compulsory,* 27 J. Legal Educ. 110 (1975); Bergen, *Report on Continuing Legal Education In Massachusetts,* 59 Mass. L.Q. 367 (1974).

Huber, *Assuring Attorney Competency: What Is to Be Done?,* 40 Tex. B.J. 215 (1977).

45. *Report of the Special Committee on Specialization and Specialized Legal Education,* 79 A.B.A. Rep. 582, 588 (1954).

46. In Rolfstad, Winkjer, Suess, McKennett and Kaiser v. Hanson, 221 N.W.2d 734, 738 (N.D. 1974) the court observed: "We do not suggest that either side is without sin in this matter. If there had been a greater degree of communication between lawyer and client, or clients, this matter may never have resulted in litigation." Very, *The Human Element in The Attorney-Client Relationship: The Answer to Malpractice,* 48 Pa. B. Ass'n Q. 515 (1977).

47. *E.g.,* in Glenna v. Sullivan, 310 Minn. 162, 245 N.W.2d 869 (1976), the court noted that many of the clients' complaints concerned inadequate attention, such as the failure to return their telephone calls and to spend sufficient time in preparing them for trial.

is frequently the primary cause of a suit for professional negligence, is usually created by carelessness in handling the attorney-client relationship. Even if the case is competently and expeditiously handled, inadequate communication may create the opposite impression.

There are few absolute values in life; most situations involve comparisons with some point of reference. This is certainly true in the field of law. Most clients form their expectations regarding the result of a legal transaction based upon the advice given them by their attorneys. If the client's hopes are raised high enough, the best any attorney can do is to meet the expectations. Although attorneys certainly owe a duty to their clients to evaluate a matter fairly and not to be overly pessimistic merely to serve their own purposes, neither the client nor the attorney is well served by projecting an outcome which is not reasonably attainable.

Realistically adjusting the client's expectations requires not only a proper evaluation of the matter, but also the exercise of care in the manner in which the client is apprised. Promises and representations which are made to a client may lay the foundation for a cause of action for breach of contract or warranty. If promises or predictions are necessary, they should be appropriately qualified. For example, if an attorney believes that there is a 60 percent chance of obtaining a certain result, he should explain to the client this means that, on the same facts and law, he would obtain a less favorable result 40 times out of 100. Make sure the client understands that there is only *one* bet, not 100. In no event should the client be left with the understanding that there has been a guarantee of success. If the client is left with that impression, it may be the basis of a complaint.

There are numerous disciplinary rules and ethical considerations which require undivided loyalty on the part of the attorney.[48] Breach of that duty may also support a malpractice claim.[49] The smallest error can be magnified out of proportion if the client perceives that it is due to a lack of loyalty.

Even if a breach of a fiduciary obligation is not serious enough to constitute malpractice, it may still disrupt the attorney-client relationship and result in a claim. The most common fiduciary problem occurs when an attorney, regardless of his motives, attempts to represent multiple parties who have actual or potential differing interests. The attorney should not undertake or continue any representation where the differing interests of the clients prevent undivided loyalty to and competent representation of each client. In any event, all existing limitations on the attorney's ability to properly represent the clients should be disclosed in writing. The clients' consent should also be secured in writing. Otherwise, multiple representations can make the attorney a quasi-guarantor for all parties.[50]

48. *E.g.,* ABA Code of Professional Responsibility, EC 5–2 through EC 5–13 and DR 5–101, 103 and 104.

49. *See* Chapter 6, Mallen & Levit; Wolfram, *supra* note 15.

50. *See* Hill v. Okay Constr. Co., 312 Minn. 324, 252 N.W.2d 107 (1977).

The attorney should usually refrain from representing both parties to a divorce, and should avoid representing more than one party in a real property transaction. An attorney retained by an insurance company to defend its insured owes the latter the same (and in some instances more) fidelity and responsibility as he owes to the entity which pays his bills.

The attorney should not represent a client if he has any personal or adverse interest which may impair his obligation of undivided loyalty and competent representation. Even where the adverse interest does not preclude fidelity and competence, the attorney should make full disclosure in writing of the potential adverse interest and its possible effect. He should also secure the client's written consent. Similarly, the attorney should disclose, in writing, the interest of any former or existing clients which may affect or limit the quality or extent of representation.[51] Of course, this requires the consent of such former or existing clients. If it cannot be obtained, an actual conflict probably is present.

The attorney should not enter into any business transaction with the client without assuring that the client receives truly independent legal advice concerning the adverse interests and the transaction itself. If legal advice is to be achieved without sending the client to another law firm, the advice should be set forth in writing and acknowledged by the client. Essentially all jurisdictions hold that there is a presumption of unfairness as to economic consideration received by an attorney from a client in a business transaction.[52]

It is imperative that the attorney preserve the client's confidences and secrets. The failure to do so, regardless of motive, can destroy the trust between the attorney and client and, of course, form an independent basis for liability.

2. *Communication*

The rapport which supports and maintains the trust in the attorney-client relationship depends upon communication. There are a number of methods of communication, but as a rule any form of communication is better than none. Telephone conferences can often be a substitute for a personal conference. Forwarding a pleading with a commercial stamp on it which simply says "reviewed by attorney A and forwarded on January 1, 1980," while not as polished or effective as dictating an analytical cover letter, is significantly better than not communicating. Even forwarding copies of pleadings without a cover letter or stamp, if explained properly in advance, is a form of communication which can also enhance your image for cost consciousness. It is important to remember that to many clients such mundane procedures as depositions or interrogatories reflect

---

51. *See* Sections 95, 103, 257, 263 and 374, Mallen & Levit.

52. *E.g.,* Flanagan v. DeLapp, 533 S.W.2d 592 (Mo. 1976); Calzada v. Sin-

the effort and the type of services for which the attorney was hired, as well as diligence to the client's case.[53]

Correspondence can take many forms. In addition to the more familiar ones, form letters can be used which permit the attorney to check off or briefly indicate what was done without the necessity of dictating a letter and waiting for it to be typed and reread. In fact, such forms are commonly used by some insurance companies in communicating with their attorneys.

The need for communication varies from the permissive to the compulsory. Many states have statutes which require authority from the client to enter into certain agreements, such as settlements.[54] Similarly, ethical considerations dictate that the client have the ultimate authority to make decisions, such as whether to accept a settlement or waive a particular defense.[55]

The failure of attorneys to advise their clients of risks and to obtain their consent prior to undertaking actions or entering into agreements has produced a significant amount of malpractice litigation. The unauthorized appearance by defense counsel, the unauthorized consent to a judgment, and the unauthorized dismissal or release of adverse parties must all be avoided because such actions change the client's legal rights and duties.

The broad area of permissive communication is governed by rules of courtesy and good sense. Thus, it is important to return telephone calls promptly. If you cannot do so personally, ask your secretary, a paralegal or another attorney in your firm to do so. Even if no one else is able to provide complete assistance, it is important that the client not feel ignored.

Always forward copies of pleadings and corporate documents which have significant impact upon the client's position. Provide your client with periodic written status reports, even if a particular report merely explains why no progress has been made since the last report. Most clients will understand postponements and cancellations, but they cannot reconcile a lack of communication with competent representation.

If communication is not effective, the best handled legal matter can produce a discontented client. If the result is not favorable, the discontent can lead to a malpractice claim even if the result obtained was as good or better than any other attorney could have achieved. In contrast, frequent communication will help build the type of relationship which may cause a client not to pursue a malpractice claim even where an error does occur.

clair, 6 Cal.App.3d 903, 86 Cal.Rptr. 387 (1970).

53. *See generally*, Smith & Nester, *Lawyers, Clients and Communication Skill,* 1977 B.Y.U. L.Rev. 275.

54. *E.g.,* Ga. Code Ann. § 9–606 (1973) (regarding settlement).

55. This is qualified somewhat by DR 7–101(B)(1) which states that a "lawyer may [w]here permissible exercise his professional judgment to waive or fail to assert a right or a position of his client." But what is "permissible"?

B. Judicial Intervention

Legal malpractice may occur in the courtroom. Errors go uncorrected because opposing counsel usually has no interest in pointing out a mistake and, in deference to the concept of the adversary process, a judge will rarely intervene in a civil proceeding to assist a party whose counsel has demonstrated incompetence. However, there are several exceptions to this rule which are the subject of this section.

A prime area of judicial concern is the competence of attorneys who undertake to represent a class in litigation. Courts have insisted that an attorney be competent before he can represent a class.[56] In one case, a judge refused to permit an attorney to represent a class because he did not understand the Federal Rules of Civil Procedure and because he was a member of the class.[57] Another area of judicial intervention is where courts observe attorneys committing a breach of their fiduciary obligations, usually by attempting to represent differing or conflicting interests.[58]

For example, one appellate court held that an attorney committed fraud on the court in a divorce action where he purported to represent the wife during trial while also representing the husband. Since the trial judge should not have permitted such representation to continue, the judgment was vacated.[59] Similarly, where an attorney switched sides in a lawsuit after being fired by his client, the court concluded that he should have withdrawn when his former client objected. When the attorney failed to withdraw voluntarily, the trial judge should have so ordered.[60] This rule has also been applied to a corporation's former attorney who subsequently undertook to represent shareholders in a derivative suit against his former client.[61] Finally, courts may achieve justice by doing their own legal research, despite the fact that an attorney failed to provide an adequate brief.[62]

Another form of judicial intervention, the imposition of sanctions upon the attorney, is preventative and remedial only prospectively. For example, in reviewing an appeal, one court imposed sanctions upon the client's attorney, payable to the adversary, because the attorney failed to deter his client from pursuing an unnecessary and frivolous appeal.[63]

56. *E.g.,* Shields v. Valley Nat'l Bank of Arizona, 56 F.R.D. 448, 449 (D. Ariz. 1971).

57. *Id.*

58. General Motors Corp. v. City of New York, 501 F.2d 639 (2d Cir. 1974); Shields v. Valley Nat'l Bank of Arizona, 56 F.R.D. 448 (D. Ariz. 1971); Laskey Bros. v. Warner Bros. Pictures, 224 F.2d 824 (2d Cir. 1955), *cert. denied* 350 U.S. 932, 76 S.Ct. 300 (1956); Bose v. Wehrli, 186 Misc. 325, 60 N.Y.S.2d 213 (1945).

59. Holmes v. Holmes, 145 Ind.App. 52, 248 N.E.2d 564 (1969); *but see,* People v. Marrero, 87 Misc.2d 563, 386 N.Y. S.2d 753 (1976).

60. Holmes v. Holmes, *supra* note 59.

61. Northeastern Okl. Community Development Corp. v. Adams, 510 P.2d 939 (Okl. 1973).

62. Slater v. Rimar, Inc., 462 Pa. 138, 338 A.2d 584 (1975).

63. In re Milch's Marriage, 47 Cal. App.3d 666, 120 Cal.Rptr. 901 (1975).

C. Administrative Intervention

1. *Administrative Agencies*

In adjudicatory hearings, administrative law judges and examiners have essentially the same latitude as federal or state court judges to intercede to prevent malpractice claims. They are not required to rely on the legal arguments of counsel or on the briefs submitted. They may undertake independent research, especially if they believe that the research submitted is inadequate. In the area of differing interests, they may hear motions that an attorney, usually for the defense, should be precluded from representing multiple clients.

For example, in *In re Merrill Lynch, Fenner & Smith, Inc.,*[64] the SEC contended that the opposing attorney had a conflict of interests concerning the representation of both Merrill Lynch and certain employees. The motion to disqualify was denied, but the order was conditioned on the requirement that the individual clients be made aware of potential conflicts and make an informed decision. To ensure this, the order was sent to each individual respondent.

2. *Professional Disciplinary Agencies*

The Clark Report[65] which reviewed the disciplinary systems in each state, listed 36 problem areas and specified recommendations for reform. The report concluded that there existed "a scandalous situation" and that "[w]ith few exceptions the prevailing attitude of lawyers towards disciplinary enforcement ranges from apathy to outright hostility. Disciplinary actions are practically nonexistent in many jurisdictions . . . ."[66]

Disciplinary boards and agencies have primarily concerned themselves with the enforcement of disciplinary rules by imposing sanctions for the violations. To some extent, this focus on deviance control can prevent malpractice claims. If clients perceive disciplinary boards as willing to investigate complaints of neglect, and likely to impose sanctions, the disciplinary mechanism will constitute a deterrent to the type of conduct which results in malpractice claims.

For example, disciplinary sanctions can be imposed for neglect and abandonment of a client's case. However, many state disciplinary boards and agencies do not investigate complaints of neglect and abandonment,[67] even though most have the power to do so.[68] This is an important area for administrative intervention, since neglect constitutes a primary cause of client complaints to disciplinary boards.[69]

---

64. SEC File No. 3–4329, unpublished opinion (Dec. 6, 1973).

65. American Bar Association Special Committee on Evaluation of Disciplinary Enforcement (Tom C. Clark, Chairman), Problems and Recommendations in Disciplinary Enforcement (Final Draft, June 1970).

66. *Id.* at 1.

67. *See* Marks & Cathcart, *Discipline Within the Legal Profession: Is It Self-Regulation?*, 1974 U.Ill. L.F. 193, 229–30.

68. ABA Code of Professional Responsibility, DR 6–101(A)(3). Unfortunately, not all states adopted this provision.

69. The annual report for the Committee on Grievances of the Association of the

In addition to regulation of the legal profession through deviance control, administrative supervision and dispute management models both offer additional preventative qualities.[70] The California certification plan for specialization is one example of administrative supervision which has a preventative purpose. The assumption is that this plan will promote increased procedural and substantive competence within those fields of law which are open to certification.

The Minnesota continuing legal education plan is another example of administrative supervision. A further step would be to institute a testing program so that the impact of the continuing legal education could be more accurately determined.

The dispute management model for regulation of the legal profession is discussed below in the section on preventing malpractice litigation. While it does involve qualities which permit it to be discussed under the heading of preventing malpractice claims, the dispute management function comes into play in most instances only after a potential malpractice claim has arisen.

D. Undoing Malpractice

1. *Introduction*

Courts are frequently asked by clients to undo forfeitures and disabilities which have been imposed because of their attorney's neglect. However, to hold a client responsible for his attorney's misconduct is merely to follow ordinary rules of agency, which dictate that the principal-client should be accountable for the attorney-agent's conduct. The manifestation of this rule is often found in the context of violations of statutory deadlines and court rules. The attorney's negligence in disregarding procedural requirements may result in the loss of his client's cause of action or defense. While the consequences of such violations can be avoided if the court consents, the client must pursue his remedy against the attorney for legal malpractice if the consent is withheld.

The attitude of the courts varies according to the nature of the error, whether there will be prejudice to an adverse party, and the effect upon judicial administration. Most jurisdictions have a statutory scheme regulating such requests.

No attempt has been made in the following sections to examine all of the numerous types of errors and consequences from which clients have sought relief. However, one generalization can safely be made: the courts usually hold the client responsible for the acts and omissions of his attorney-agent, offering the client as solace the suggestion that he sue his attorney for legal malpractice.[71]

Bar of the City of New York (1967–68) stated that over half of the 2,232 complaints involved neglect. N.Y.L.J., Sept. 12, 1968, at 4, col. 5.

70. This topic was one of the central themes discussed in Steele & Nimmer, *supra* note 9, at 1008.

71. In Brown v. E. W. Bliss Co., 72 F.R.D. 198 (D. Md. 1976), the court

2. *Unauthorized Appearance*

Clients have often urged courts to grant relief because their attorneys acted in excess of or without any authority. Most reported decisions concern clients who requested relief from a default judgment which occurred after the attorney voluntarily appeared even though process had not been served, or where the attorney consented to a judgment without the client's consent. Despite protests of the client that the attorney did not have sufficient authority for such an act, the courts have usually refused to grant relief.[72] The primary consideration militating against undoing the attorney's malpractice as to one client is that it will adversely affect another party who is at least as innocent.

Courts have not been totally insensitive to the client's dilemma. In referring the client to his remedy against the attorney, most courts have first determined that the remedy exists. Thus, if the client is to be bound because of the attorney's negligence or unauthorized acts, the courts have indicated that the client must be a resident,[73] the attorney solvent,[74] and that there be no appearance of fraud.[75]

There is no great unfairness in binding the client where his attorney acts in *excess of* his actual authority. Ordinary agency rules hold that an innocent party should not be prejudiced where he justifiably relies upon the agent's apparent authority. In one jurisdiction, this rule has been applied even though the "client" claimed and demonstrated that he never retained or even heard of the attorney who purported to act on his behalf.[76]

The better view recognizes that one cannot be bound by the representations of a purported agent where no agency exists. In these jurisdictions, the plaintiff can show the absence of the agency relationship to establish that the judgment was rendered without jurisdiction over his person.[77] The party seeking relief must also show that he is free from any fault in the situation which is at issue.[78]

3. *Default Judgment*

A common source of malpractice litigation results from the attorney's failure to appear for and defend his client. Clients have generally had

urged judges to stop being solicitous of attorneys, especially where the client would sustain no loss because he could sue the attorney. The court opined that in relation to other professionals, attorneys are not sued often enough for malpractice. This was cited as another consideration for denying relief. *Cf.* Friedman v. Jablonski, 371 Mass. 482, 358 N.E.2d 994 (1976) (failure to discover misrepresentations as to title). Martin v. Cook, 68 Cal.App.3d 799, 137 Cal.Rptr. 434 (1977). For a detailed discussion of the various policy considerations, *see Negligent Litigation and Relief from Judgments: The Case for a Second Chance,* 50 S.Cal.L.Rev. 1207 (1977).

72. *E.g.,* In re Hamilton's Estate, 81 Misc.2d 40, 364 N.Y.S.2d 950 (1974).

73. *E.g.,* Petker v. Rudolph, 168 Misc. 909, 6 N.Y.S.2d 296, aff'd 258 App.Div. 1040, 17 N.Y.S.2d 1020 (1938).

74. *Id.*

75. Munnikuyson's Adm'x v. Dorsett's Adm'x, 2 Har.&G. 374 (Md.1828).

76. *E.g.,* Abbott & Co. v. Dutton, 44 Vt. 546, 8 Am.Rep. 394 (1872).

77. *E.g.,* Reynolds v. Fleming, 30 Kan. 106, 1 P. 61 (1883).

78. Jones v. Williamson Adm'r, 45 Tenn. (5 Cold) 371 (1868).

very little success in their efforts to set aside a judgment entered because of their attorney's absence. Instead, courts have suggested that the clients sue their attorneys.[79]

There are jurisdictional variations as to whether and when a client may seek relief from the consequences of any such negligence.[80] The views range from one extreme, that the attorney's negligence can never be a basis for relief,[81] to the other, where the clients can urge their own innocence in exculpation.[82]

The intermediate view is most common and has several components. The negligence of an attorney will not be imputed where to do so would amount to a fraud on his client.[83] For example, the unauthorized withdrawal from, or abandonment of, a case by an attorney can operate as a fraud.[84] A predominant, and often statutory, position is that a default can be avoided where there is excusable neglect.[85] The attorney's error may be excusable if it was attributable to an honest mistake, an accident, or other cause which is not inconsistent with reasonable diligence.[86] Inattentiveness has not been held to so qualify,[87] such as where the error was the failure to calendar the trial date.[88] By the same token, an attorney's error in judgment, in failing to assert a defense, has been held not to constitute excusable neglect.[89] Some jurisdictions have statutes which also permit the court to award the opposing party costs or expenses occasioned by an attorney's negligence, or even fine the attorney a specified amount.[90]

4. Failure to Prosecute or Comply with Procedure

Another common basis for malpractice by the litigation attorney is the failure to comply with procedural deadlines and requirements. Such an error can result in the action being dismissed for a violation of court rules or orders.[91]

The prevailing view is that the client is charged with his attorney's neglect and must bear the consequences. This view was expressed by the

---

79. *E.g.,* Tarloff v. Werner, 72 Misc.2d 26, 337 N.Y.S.2d 916 (1972); Universal Film Exchanges, Inc. v. Lust, 479 F.2d 573 (4th Cir. 1973).

80. *E.g.,* Kuhn v. Indiana Ice & Fuel Co., 104 Ind.App. 387, 11 N.E.2d 508 (1937); Newman, Northrup, Levinson & Becker v. Schueck, 58 Ill.App. 328 (1895).

81. Vincent v. Kelly, 121 Okl. 302, 249 P. 942 (1926).

82. *See* White v. Sadler, 350 Mich. 511, 87 N.W.2d 192 (1957); Newman, Northrup, Levinson & Becker v. Schueck, 58 Ill.App. 328 (1895).

83. Ingalls v. Arbeiter, 72 S.D. 488, 36 N.W.2d 669 (1949).

84. *Id.* In Perkins v. Sykes, 233 N.C. 147, 63 S.E.2d 133 (1951), the withdrawal of counsel without notice to his client constituted "surprise" under the applicable statute, thus permitting the judgment to be set aside.

85. Kivett v. Crouch, 61 Idaho 536, 104 P.2d 21 (1940) (mistake, inadvertence, surprise or excusable neglect); Robinson v. Varela, 67 Cal.App.3d 611, 136 Cal.Rptr. 783 (1977) (excuse found).

86. Williams v. Knox, 10 N.J.Super. 384, 76 A.2d 712 (1950).

87. *Id.*

88. Tarloff v. Werner, 72 Misc.2d 26, 337 N.Y.S.2d 916 (1972).

89. Penryn Land Co. v. Akahori, 37 Cal. App. 14, 173 P. 612 (1918).

90. Kivett v. Crouch, 61 Idaho 536, 104 P.2d 21 (1940).

91. Lange v. Hickman, 92 Nev. 41, 544 P.2d 1208 (1976) (failure to comply with discovery order).

United States Supreme Court in *Link v. Wabash R.R.,*[92] which concerned the propriety of a federal district court's dismissal on the ground that the attorney had failed to appear for a pre-trial conference. The Supreme Court concluded that, under our judicial system, agency principles compel that a client be held responsible for the acts and omissions of his chosen attorney. The client's remedy is not to undo the advantage received by his adversary, but to sue his own attorney.[93] This view has been followed by lower federal courts.[94] An additional rationale is that "strict compliance with the rules is necessary if we [the courts] are to achieve our goal of current calendars."[95]

There is an incongruity in expediting court calendars by penalizing clients for their attorneys' negligence. Pragmatically, the relative efficiency of the calendar remains unchanged since a "current" calendar is achieved only by adding legal malpractice actions to future calendars. It can be argued, however, that holding the client accountable will prevent other malpractice.

Perhaps with this consideration in mind, the Fifth Circuit has ameliorated the *Link v. Wabash R.R.* view, in a case where, unlike the dilatory tactics in *Link,* the attorney had not proceeded in bad faith.[96] The attorney had appeared on the day of trial announcing that he had discovered new evidence and needed to amend the complaint. The district court refused. The attorney requested a dismissal without prejudice. The court again refused and counsel stated that he could not proceed with the trial. The court dismissed the action with prejudice.

The Fifth Circuit initially observed that "the effect of the dismissal was to visit the sins of the lawyer upon his client."[97] The attorney may have been negligent in failing to discover the new evidence sooner. He may have been inconsiderate of the waiting witnesses, opposing counsel, and the trial judge with his last-minute announcement. But since his good faith was assumed, he was entitled to urge his client's interest and refuse to proceed. The relief requested, a dismissal without prejudice, was not unreasonable, since at worst it merely subjected the adversary to a second lawsuit. The dismissal with prejudice was held to be improper.[98]

The state courts have expressed a diversity of views.[99] In one case, the negligence of the attorney in prosecuting the action was so gross as to

---

92. 370 U.S. 626, 82 S.Ct. 1386 (1962). The attorney had called the clerk with the excuse that he had to file papers with the Illinois Supreme Court. The federal judge was unimpressed.

93. *Id.* at 634, note 10.

94. Brown v. E. W. Bliss Co., 72 F.R.D. 198 (D. Md. 1976); Quagliano v. United States, 293 F.Supp. 670 (S.D.N.Y. 1968) (failure to appear for trial). *See also* Walker Int'l Corp. v. United States, 554 F.2d 64 (1977).

95. Quagliano v. United States, 293 F.Supp. 670, 672 (S.D.N.Y. 1968).

96. Durham v. Florida East Coast Ry. Co., 385 F.2d 366 (5th Cir. 1967).

97. *Id.* at 367.

98. *Id. See also* Flaksa v. Little River Marine Constr. Co., 389 F.2d 885 (5th Cir. 1968), *cert. denied* 392 U.S. 928, 88 S.Ct. 2287 (1968).

99. *See* Annot., *Attorney's Inaction as Excuse for Failure to Timely Prosecute Action,* 15 A.L.R.3d 674; Annot., *Pretrial Conference—Failure to Appear,* 55 A.L.R.3d 303. *E.g.,* Estate of Gasbarini v. Medical Center of Beaver County, 253 Pa.Super. 547, 385 A.2d 474 (1978);

deprive his client of effective representation and entitle her to relief from the dismissal.[100]   A salutary alternative may be available, by penalizing the attorney with a fine for his negligence and not the client.[101]   Of course, if the attorney's error is attributable to the negligence of the court or clerk, the client will not be penalized.[102]

Section III

PREVENTING MALPRACTICE LITIGATION

A. Introduction

Once a malpractice claim is presented, there may an alternative to litigation which will achieve a fair, expeditious and economical result for both the attorney and the client.   Arbitration, which has been used with some success, may be a viable alternative to legal malpractice litigation. Under some circumstances the benefits of a client security fund may be available without the need for litigation.   However, the absence of a viable civil remedy is usually a condition precedent for receiving such assistance.

Regardless of the availability of such procedural devices and remedies, the attorney can always consider self-help.   The goals of self-help are to either preserve the attorney-client relationship or to prevent those who once shared a common objective from becoming public adversaries.   The tools of self-help are primarily the negotiating skills and knowledge of the attorney and his ability to rationally analyze his own degree of fault.

B. Arbitration

1. *Medical*

Malpractice problems confronted physicians earlier than attorneys. For this reason, arbitration of medical malpractice claims has already received significant attention[103] while arbitration of legal malpractice claims has not.[104]

Martin v. Cook, 68 Cal.App.3d 799, 137 Cal.Rptr. 434 (1977) (error not excused).

100. Daley v. County of Butte, 227 Cal. App.2d 380, 38 Cal.Rptr. 693 (1964); *see also* Kamp v. Syracuse Transit Corp., 284 App.Div. 1028, 134 N.Y.S.2d 919 (1954), *appeal denied* 285 App.Div. 859, 137 N.Y.S.2d 851 (1955); *but see* Brock v. Fouchy, 76 Cal.App.2d 363, 172 P.2d 945 (1946).

101. Sommer v. Fucci, 47 A.D.2d 771, 365 N.Y.S.2d 249 (1975).

102. Kizer v. Martin, 132 So.2d 14 (Fla. App. 1961).

103. Nocas, *Arbitration of Medical Malpractice Claims,* 13 The Forum 254 (1977); Berkman, *Alternatives to Medical Malpractice Litigation,* 12 The Forum 479 (1977); Epstein, *Medical Malpractice: The Case for Contract,* 1976 A.B.F. Res. J. 87, 136–38; Lerner, *Arbitration of Professional and Institutional Liability Claims,* 1976 The Forum 484; *Medical Malpractice: Report of Department of Health, Education, and Welfare,* the Secretary's Commission on Medical Malpractice (Washington, D.C., 1973).

104. The author is aware of instances where the parties to legal malpractice litigation have agreed to arbitration and

Pilot projects at various hospitals, primarily on the West Coast, have adopted arbitration clauses to resolve disputes between patients, physicians and hospitals.[105] Most of these programs permit the patient to reject the arbitration agreement, both prior to receiving medical attention, and within 30 days after leaving the clinic or hospital. As long as such agreements are not executed by patients who are seriously ill or in need of immediate medical attention, these arbitration provisions are probably enforceable.[106]

Two recent statutory attempts to require a form of arbitration did not fair as well. Illinois enacted a statute which created a medical malpractice review panel with three members: a judge, an attorney and a doctor. The panel was obligated to convene upon the filing of a medical malpractice claim. However, even though the panel had the power to make conclusions of law and fact, the findings were not admissible and the parties were not bound in any way by the panel's decision unless the parties unanimously agreed.

In *Wright v. Central Du Page Hospital Ass'n,*[107] the Illinois Supreme Court held the Illinois statute unconstitutional because it provided that a judge could be overruled by persons who are not members of the judiciary. In addition, it constituted an impediment to the right of a trial by jury. Another problem, not discussed in the Illinois decision, is that the judge sitting on the panel later hears the case if the parties do not agree to be bound, possibly impairing his impartiality. In contrast to the Illinois decision, the constitutionality of a similar New York statute was sustained on appeal following an adverse decision by the trial court.[108]

These decisions demonstrate that statutory arbitration can be instituted. However, it is clear that attempts to legislate barriers between patients and physicians will receive close scrutiny.

2. *Legal*

In the legal malpractice area, it is likely that any such attempt would receive even closer scrutiny. The fiduciary obligations of attorneys militate against the validity of an arbitration provision and may result in it being held presumptively void. Ethical constraints dictate that arbitration agreements may only be permissible if the client is given the opportunity to consult with an independent attorney.[109]

If permissible, contractual arbitration provisions hold some promise for preventing legal malpractice litigation. Agreements for arbitration can

---

malpractice carriers engage in arbitration to resolve coverage disputes. However, no scholarly attention appears to have been given to the subject.

105. *See* Lerner, *supra* note 103.

106. *See* Doyle v. Giuliucci, 62 Cal.2d 606, 43 Cal.Rptr. 697, 401 P.2d 1 (1965).

107. 63 Ill.2d 313, 347 N.E.2d 736 (1976).

108. *See* Comiskey v. Arlen, 55 A.D.2d 304, 390 N.Y.S.2d 122 (1976). A Flori-

da mandatory panel survived a constitutional attack in Carter v. Sparkman, 335 So.2d 802 (Fla. 1976), *cert. denied* 429 U.S. 1041, 97 S.Ct. 740 (1977). *See also,* Bogart & Kinzie, Challenge to Malpractice Screening Panels, INCL Brief, Nov. 1977, at 16.

109. Formal Opinion No. 1977–47, Comm. Professional Ethics, 53 Cal. St. B.J. 338 (1978).

be made at the same time representation is first accepted or after a malpractice claim is made. However, most attorneys would correctly perceive that combining an initial discussion of the client's legal problem together with the resolution of a potential malpractice claim by arbitration would cause the client to seek another attorney.

Once a malpractice claim is made, though, there is little, if any, damage which can be done to the attorney-client relationship by suggesting that the dispute be arbitrated. However, the attorney should confer with his liability carrier to be sure he is not breaching the cooperation clause of the insurance policy. While views are changing, most claims managers are not in favor of arbitration of legal malpractice claims.

The attorney must remember that any agreement made during the attorney-client relationship, including one for arbitration, is subject to fiduciary obligations and the presumption of voidability. But, if the arbitration agreement is achieved in an ethical manner, it can benefit both parties. First, the dispute will probably be resolved in a significantly shorter period of time than by litigation. Second, the cost in terms of legal fees, expenses and time is likely to be significantly reduced. Third, an arbitration proceeding will probably be less emotionally charged and may offer some opportunity to maintain or at least resume professional contact afterward.

The question of which party arbitration is more likely to benefit is perhaps the most important consideration for both clients and attorneys. Most clients would prefer to try their case before a jury, while most attorneys would probably prefer to have a court act as the trier of fact. Arbitration falls somewhere in between.

3. *Professional Disciplinary Agencies*

As discussed earlier in this Chapter, disciplinary boards and agencies have the ability to resolve differences between attorneys and clients. The arbitration of fee disputes is one example where such intervention can be effective. Many bar associations have committees or panels which hear and rule on voluntarily submitted disputes.[110]

The potential for preventing malpractice litigation through the efforts of committees and panels connected with bar associations is presently limited by the public's perception that such organizations are either uninterested, ineffective or biased in favor of attorneys. There is nothing, however, which prevents bar associations from improving this image and establishing a viable alternative to civil litigation.

110. Special Committee on Resolution of Fee Disputes of the American Bar Association Section of Bar Activities, *The Resolution of Fee Disputes: A Report and Model By-Laws* 4 (1974); Lewis, *Fee Dispute Determination—The Alle-* *gheny County Experience,* 121 Pitt. Leg. J. 3 (July, 1973); Bodle, *The Arbitration of Fee Disputes Between Attorneys and Clients,* 38 L.A.B. Bull. 265 (1963).

C. Security Funds

Client security funds may also be an alternative to litigation. These funds are implemented by the state supreme court and administered by the state bar.[111] The California Client Security Fund is typical of the plans adopted in most jurisdictions.[112]

A prerequisite for payment is that the loss was caused by the "dishonest conduct" of an attorney, while acting as an attorney or in a fiduciary capacity incidental to the practice of law.[113] Generally, the loss must concern money or property which was in the attorney's possession. Recovery is not permitted if the attorney has liability insurance or if the applicant has indemnity insurance. Moreover, the applicant must first recover a judgment against the attorney or show the attorney's death, mental incompetency, resignation from the practice of law, or criminal conviction. In California, payment is a matter of "grace and not right," being within the sole discretion of the state bar.[114] Recovery cannot exceed a specified maximum amount per transaction.[115]

Client security funds are generally financed by voluntary contributions from members of the bar and/or the transfer of funds derived from attorneys' state licensing fees. Thus far, client security funds have survived various constitutional attacks.[116]

D. Self-Help

When a client complains about the handling of a legal matter, one option is to take direct measures to prevent the filing of a malpractice lawsuit. Of course, if the client's dissatisfaction first appears in a complaint, the options are limited to settlement or litigation.

It is a serious mistake for an attorney to undertake, without some independent advice, the defense or negotiation of a malpractice claim directed against him or his firm. Before undertaking self-help, in order not to imperil professional liability coverage, an attorney should first provide notice to the liability carrier.[117]

---

111. *See,* Outcault, Jr. & Petersen, *Lawyer Discipline and Professional Standards in California: Progress and Problems,* 24 Hastings L.J. 675 (1973); Standing Committee on Clients' Security Fund, *Report,* 96 A.B.A. Rep. 595 (1971); Bryan, *Clients' Security Fund Ten Years Later,* 55 A.B.A.J. 757 (1969).

112. Cal. Bus. & Prof. Code § 6140.5 and Rules of Procedure, Rules 102 to 120. *See also, e.g.,* In re Client Security Fund, 254 Ark. 1075, 493 S.W.2d 422 (1973).

113. Cal. Rules of Procedure, Rule 103. *E.g.,* Folly Farms I Inc. v. Trustees of the Clients' Sec. Trust Fund of the Bar of Md., 282 Md. 659, 387 A.2d 248 (1978); Whittier Union High Sch. Dist.

v. Superior Court, 66 Cal.App.3d 504, 136 Cal.Rptr. 86 (1977).

114. Cal. Rules of Procedure, Rule 115.

115. Cal. Rules of Procedure, Rule 114 ($25,000). The Arkansas plan has a $5,000 limit. *See* In re Client Security Fund, 254 Ark. 1075, 493 S.W.2d 422 (1973).

116. *E.g.,* Hagopian v. Justices of Supreme Judicial Court, 429 F.Supp. 367 (D. Mass. 1977); Bennett v. Oregon State Bar, 256 Or. 37, 470 P.2d 945 (1970).

117. Some carriers will undertake the expense of retaining an attorney to assist in undoing the problem or in mitigating damages.

In any discussion with the client concerning the nature of the problem and possible remedies, it is important to document the fact that such discussions are part of an attempt to settle a dispute. Otherwise, the attorney risks making admissions against his own interest which, if the matter is not settled, may be urged as evidence of liability at trial. If the case may be brought in federal court, even greater care is required because of the liberalized provisions on discovery of factual statements made during settlement negotiations.[118]

In addition, when a client raises a problem, it is important to distinguish between a settlement of the potential malpractice claim and a settlement or correction of the underlying problem itself. Any attempt to cover up the underlying problem will create a separate cause of action.[119]

Despite these potential problems, self-help can prevent malpractice litigation even where a valid malpractice claim exists. Ideally, the primary form of self-help would be an attempt to undo or mitigate the effect of the attorney's negligence. If the attorney does not possess the knowledge or skill required for the task, he should seek assistance from another attorney or from his liability carrier.

If the injury cannot be undone or mitigated, an initial obstacle to self-help may be that the client no longer has confidence in the original attorney handling the matter. Transferring responsibility for the work may be of some assistance. The fees and expenses for work which is being questioned, whether or not billed or paid, can be offered as a subject for negotiation. A monetary settlement should be considered, but if the attorney expects the settlement to be paid or reimbursed by his liability carrier, he must have its consent.

In order to implement any aspect of the self-help remedy effectively, some degree of rapport must exist with the client. To retain whatever rapport remains after the client asserts a malpractice claim, it is important for attorneys to recognize that a client's perception that an error occurred is not necessarily illogical, even where negligence has not occurred. Few clients understand that whether an error occurred and whether it was negligent are separate issues. Preparation is required to discuss a client's perception that an error occurred, while trying to focus the client's attention on the difference between the possible existence of an error and the question of whether that error was negligent. If it does not rise well above a defensive argument, it is not worth pursuing.

118. Federal Rule of Evidence 408.
119. Mitchell v. Transamerica Ins. Co., 551 S.W.2d 586 (Ky. App. 1977) (the malpractice insurer participated in the deception).

Chapter 2

WORK CONTROL

L. Don Holland
and
Jeffrey M. Smith

Section I

INTRODUCTION

No attempt has been made to cover the wide spectrum of different work control systems. To do so would not only prevent the text from being condensed to a readable length, it would also fail as an attempt to prescribe a system for each firm. Rather, the overview in Chapter 1 and the analysis of details in Chapter 2 are designed to enable each firm to more effectively design a system which will be suitable for its own particular needs.

A division has been made between the two major aspects of work control: the conflict of interests and the calendar systems. While many aspects of these systems are virtually identical, there are distinctions. They also share a common problem in that attorneys in too many instances do not properly utilize the systems even after implementing them in a particular form.

As was discussed in Chapter 1, the term "conflict of interests systems" is utilized here for ease of recognition. The discussion will, however, deal with the broader area of differing interests. As defined in the ABA Code of Professional Responsibility, "differing interests" includes but is not limited to "conflicting interests."

Finally, the following discussion has been formulated to aid the widest possible audience. Certain aspects may be too fundamental for some attorneys. However, it will hopefully be utilized by attorneys, law office managers and support staff.

Section II

CONFLICT OF INTERESTS SYSTEMS

Every law firm should have an index system which includes information on clients and other parties to non-litigation matters, as well as information on all plaintiffs and defendants involved in litigation the firm is handling. The reason for establishing a client index for litigation is apparent, but the other indexes are sometimes neglected. Such indexes can be an important method of preventing a firm from representing differing or conflicting interests.

Each attorney must know whether the interest of any former or present client might affect or limit the quality or extent of representation. An attorney should not risk the chance that the interests of past, present or future clients will diverge, thereby disqualifying the attorney from representing any of them. Direct business competition may lead to a situation almost as difficult as actual litigation between clients.

It is likewise important to know whether the firm has any actions or cross-actions against a defendant whom the client wishes to sue. Without such information, various clients of the same attorney or firm may find themselves in competition for the limited resources of a defendant which are insufficient to satisfy all of the potential judgments. This type of conflict has obvious potential for producing malpractice claims. Attorneys in the same firm cannot be in a "race to the courthouse."

It is also important to know if a prospective client has been involved in a prior transaction with an existing client of the firm. If so, and if litigation were to arise in the future over any such transaction, the existing client would usually expect the firm to be in a position to proceed on his behalf. If the firm accepts a new matter without being aware of this potential conflict of interests, it may find itself prohibited from representing either client. Among other problems, the firm may be liable for the fees and expenses necessary for a succeeding firm to attain the level of knowledge of the original firm regarding the existing client.

While effective use of a conflict of interests system will assist in detecting this type of problem, a solution must also be developed. Each case will certainly involve relatively unique facts, but in all situations where a possible conflict exists between a prospective and current client, a firm must consult the existing client before undertaking the representation of the prospective client. The intention to consult the existing client must be disclosed to the prospective client. If that client objects, not only is the firm precluded from discussing the matter with the current client, but an actual conflict probably exists.

The purpose of procedures, techniques or operations (collectively a system) used to isolate a potentially differing interest is to define a law firm's relationships between current clients and potential clients. The relationships must be defined specifically enough to allow an attorney or a committee within a firm to decide if the relationships can potentially create a situation in which the interests of such clients might differ from each other.

The need to discover the potentially differing interests obviously surpasses the mere business decision to maximize profits. The Code of Professional Responsibility usually requires that an attorney and his firm should resolve doubts concerning potentially differing interests against undertaking the representation.

A. The Basic System

An attorney, all attorneys in the firm, or a committee within the firm must be given the *express* duty or responsibility of identifying the potentially differing interests. Allowing the responsibility to be an individually defined duty creates the worst possible situation. A firm may believe it has a system, thereby relaxing ad hoc safeguards, when in fact the system exists only in theory.

The most rudimentary and by far the most practiced system is the oral system. It is not without some redeeming qualities and it usually works for very small firms which are relatively new. However, the oral system is unfortunately used in firms of more than 100 years of cumulative experience and more than 20 attorneys. The system is basically word of mouth, with attorneys asking each other what is known of a particular client or matter. Failing memories and a lack of details cause a finger-walking exercise through the case files in the office. This system is unacceptable in almost all circumstances and thus does not warrant further discussion. Having such a system should be an immediate red flag, and prompt action should be taken to correct the situation.

Anyone who is not courting a malpractice case or disciplinary action will have, at a minimum, a card or index file of clients. See Figure 1. By keeping a file of client names in alphabetical order, any member of the firm can review (search) the index file and determine the existence of many potentially differing interests. There is no necessity for the responsible attorney to be present, and the search is relatively efficient and accurate compared to the oral system. However, an index which contains only client names does not yield complete information concerning potentially differing interests.

A more thorough approach utilizes the client names and includes additional information on the index cards. See Figure 2. Now a search of the information base will not only identify existing client names, but will provide additional facts about the clients that may be helpful. Including the additional information involves only an incremental increase in time and cost for the input and the search.

The needed information can be gathered from a client or matter-fact sheet, new file opening memorandum, or matter identifier memorandum (hereinafter new matter memo). See Figure 3a. With such a system, the designated or responsible attorney(s) can review the cards rapidly and efficiently without relying on the attorneys' memories and without reviewing actual files. Normally included on the card in this basic approach is the client name (indexing entry), client number, matter name, matter number, a brief matter description, caption, address, opposing party, opposing counsel, responsible attorney, and assigned attorney(s).

After identifying any potentially differing interests, an in-depth review must be made to resolve actual differing or conflicting interests. At this point, the new client or new matter may be accepted or rejected. Thus, the goal is to adopt a system which allows fast, efficient, and accurate information retrieval by attorneys or their staff. Those who initially retrieve the information may, but need not, have actual knowledge of the clients and matters under scrutiny.

B. Multiple Index Systems

The next step in developing a more comprehensive system should be apparent. The responsible attorney may want to search his information base using indexes other than client name, such as opposing party, opposing counsel, or matter description. To perform this multi-index search with a system utilizing one index card per client, at least two searches must be performed, one by reviewing or retrieving based on the client name (first key) and the second by retrieving the additional item, i.e., the matter description (second key). The second search is difficult and time consuming since *every* card must be reviewed (the information base is in client-name order or sequence).

The search and retrieval could be simplified if there were two files with the same data, one having the information arranged (sorted) by client name and one sorted by matter description. In effect, the total information base (data set) would be ordered and sorted by two methods (keys). As the data set expands in size, and the search requests expand in complexity, more keys will be added (more files in the information base) and the ways an inquiry may be made to the client information increases. See Figure 4. This system is more accurate and far more efficient than the more basic single index system. The firm's client relationships can be evaluated using different "keys". In a relatively short time, a report can be prepared on the potentially differing interests for a more detailed review.

There are sophisticated manual retrieval systems using punched holes, notches, and color coding. These features allow the storage problem caused by the duplicating of index cards to be kept to a minimum. The holes, notches, or colors allow one card to be retrieved on several keys and more information can be included on each card. The cards can be used for several purposes, e.g., conflict file, billing file, or telephone file.

Later in the Chapter, the possibilities for key information will be expanded on when discussing computerized systems. However, the basic information contained in any computer system can be included in a manual system.

The more sophisticated manual system is known as an inverted file system, where the information contained on the index card is refiled (inverted) under each key (item). The refiling or inverting of the original file enables the searcher to "go in to" (query) the file using several keys the same way one uses an index in a book. Naturally, as client information grows, the index, because it is representing many items for each client, will grow significantly faster. This growth of keys and information can indicate the need for mechanized assistance. The information suggested here is generally present in a mechanized system, but may not be inclusive for a particular situation.

The more sophisticated approaches to conflict of interests systems make use of machines to gather (input), store, selectively retrieve, maintain, and update the relevant information. The most common equipment in attorneys' offices which can handle this function is word processing equipment. Continuously, and in ever expanding numbers, word processing equipment is replacing the common typewriter. The major advantage of word processing is the storage capability. No longer are the operator's keystrokes forgotten after the element hits the paper. The stroke is stored, either in "memory" (semi-conductor chips inside the word processor) or on some magnetic storage media such as tape (like the home tape recorder), disks (either soft or hard), or cards. To retrieve the information, the word processing equipment can review (scan) the stored data in only a few seconds. Selected data can then be printed automatically from the storage media.

Not all word processing equipment can be used for a conflict of interests system. Just as manual systems differ in sophistication, so does word processing equipment. The more basic word processor will allow serial processing (one key) of the stored information. This allows the operator to review the data from the beginning of the file to the needed information, thereby employing a faster version of the simple manual system. As the word processor increases in sophistication (and price), its capability increases to search and retrieve data since multiple keys are used.

In discussing equipment, or even manual systems, it is difficult to state unequivocally that one system is "better" than another without a complete understanding of the environment of the equipment. Some of the factors to be considered are size of a firm, price of equipment, uses of equipment, time and space requirements, size of files or information to be stored, and types and abilities of operators. The selection of the correct equipment is not an easy one and should be made only with the proper knowledge of equipment, application procedures and the needs in a particular firm.

Regardless of the type of equipment chosen, the manual tasks simulated by the machine are faster, more efficient, and more accurate. In addition, the concepts in searching which are unwieldy with a manual system can be quite manageable with a machine. Word processors or computers (word processors are usually small, specifically dedicated computers) can easily handle 10, 20 or more keys. Large data sets consisting of several keys, each key representing a file of client information, can be reviewed in seconds. If the file in question involves vast amounts of data and complex searches, then a machine may be the only practical way to proceed.

Typical information which can be included in the information base to aid in identifying potentially differing interests includes: client name (here, one of many indexing entries), client number, client subsidiaries and affiliates, industry designations, matter name, matter number, a brief matter description, area of law or practice, attorney responsible for the matter, attorney responsible for the client, other parties, other party subsidiaries and affiliates, other party attorneys, court, judge, caption, court number, date file opened, date file closed, and location of file.

After a file is created, searches can be performed using the above data to identify potentially differing interests. For example, the new client and its partners, control persons, subsidiaries or affiliates, can be checked against the key file of current clients. Then the new client can be checked against the existing opposing party key file. If identical or similar names are found in the new data and the old data, "a hit" occurs. The information is then reported to the responsible attorney for a more detailed analysis. Next, the opposing party for the new client is compared to the firm's current client and existing opposite party key files. Again, a hit results in a report.

The procedures stated above are basic. Further comparisons may be made based on the type of industry, attorney, or judge, and these more subtle comparisons can also reveal potentially differing interests.

C. Information Base

A system for identifying potentially differing interests does not exist in a vacuum. Necessary forms and procedures are required so that the system, whether manual, partially automated, or totally automated, functions properly. Functioning properly is defined as having the correct and needed information in the system *and* having the proper tools to retrieve that information in a fast, efficient and accurate manner.

Definitions are not as difficult as practical considerations. How does a firm acquire and store the needed information and, once stored, how does a firm get the information back out of the system? The system must provide for a flow of information starting with the first interview of a new client or an old client with a new matter (collectively, new client matter). The resulting flow must culminate with a timely positive or negative answer to the client regarding representation.

The flow begins with an interview, whether in person, by telephone and/or written correspondence. The attorney first having contact with the new client matter (the originating attorney) must elicit as much of the needed information as possible for the search of the information base. The most logical way to do this is for the originating attorney to proceed through a list of questions (or boxes or items) on a form. The form can be written or produced on a terminal (typing device connected to a computer). See Figure 3. The information is then forwarded to a person charged with actually comparing the new information with the firm's existing information base. Rather than using forms, the firm can provide a terminal and the originating attorney himself may actually input and compare the information (query or search the information base) for differing interests.

Either directly or indirectly, the originating attorney queries the information base. Any or all of the steps may be manual and the information base may be on a three-by-five index card file or may be stored electronically on magnetic media. If a firm is using machines to store and retrieve, then one part of the system is the program(s) (set of instructions used by the computer to control the activities the machine must perform) needed to activate the query. On word processors, the software program may consist entirely of performing certain "sort" or "select" steps provided by the manufacturer. On sophisticated computers, the software program may be a complicated set of instructions devised by a programmer to fit the information base and practices of the particular firm.

The result of the query will be a report showing all potentially differing interests the new client matter brings to the firm's present clients and matters. See Figure 5. The report is then reviewed by the responsible attorney(s) or review committee. If a more detailed search is needed, it can be performed.

A diagram showing the flow of information (flow chart) is depicted in Figure 6. Note that the system information flows the same way whether or not a computer is used.

Section III

CALENDAR CONTROL SYSTEMS

A. Introduction

Law firms are continually bridled by deadlines and time requirements. Just as any business, a firm must have some system to deal with this aspect of administration. But, like the conflict of interests situation, the attorney is held to a higher degree of care than the normal businessman. Where a normal business may lose the customer or sale, a firm or attorney has the additional potential for a malpractice suit or sanction under the Code of Professional Responsibility.

Time-related errors are one of the most frequent and yet most preventable sources of malpractice claims. Procrastination in handling a client's case can easily lead to client dissatisfaction. If this involves a failure to file a pleading, to apply for a license, or take any similar step in a timely manner, it may cause damage and a malpractice claim.

All attorneys are under an ethical duty to use care to safeguard the interests of their clients [1] and not to neglect a matter entrusted to them.[2]

1. ABA Code of Professional Responsibility, EC 6–4.

2. ABA Code of Professional Responsibility, DR 6–101(A)(3).

However, even the attorney who is generally careful and does not neglect a client's affairs may inadvertently fail to comply with a time deadline unless a systems approach is applied to preventing time-related errors.

There are many basic systems, and a multitude of variations. The literature on the subject is prolix.[3] Other sources of information include law firms which have adopted systems, as well as commercial services which provide advice or programs. However, there are several factors which must be considered before implementing any system.

First, the firm's various areas of practice must be analyzed. For example, if a firm has 10 attorneys and only one engages in litigation, the appropriate calendar system for litigation matters will be quite different from the one adopted by a firm of a similar size with six litigators.

A second factor to be considered is input. No system will succeed without complete information. Although few attorneys would disagree with the proposition that a system should be used to control pleadings, documents, closings and even anticipated action or client imposed deadlines, some may rationalize that not all information need be conveyed to the person in charge of monitoring the system. One solution to the input problem is to have that person periodically spot check files. For example, an inspection can be made of pleadings which obviously need responses, such as complaints and motions, to determine if the due dates for responses were originally entered into the system. Similarly, audit inquiries and proposed closing checklists can be reviewed.

Third, someone must be designated to monitor the system. The choice of the person to monitor the system should be made on pragmatic grounds. It cannot be someone who either lacks the position or the temperament to insist on compliance with the system's procedures. Except in unusual circumstances, it must be one of the law firm's partners. In order to avoid unnecessary disputes, a comprehensive policy should be adopted to deal with persons who fail to handle matters in a timely fashion or who otherwise do not comply with the system's procedures.

Fourth, a method of ensuring compliance must be established. The system should provide written notice in advance of the internal due date. The internal due date must be early enough to permit corrective action prior to the actual deadline. If the matter is not taken care of by the internal due date, provision must be made for a report to the person in

3. Walshe, *Math/Sort Packages: New Dimensions in Word Processing*, 65 A.B.A.J. 72 (1979); O'Brien, A Docket Control and Tickler System, *Legal Economics*, Economics, Fall 1976, at 40; DeMeo, Case Control, *Calendar Reminder and Follow-up Systems*, 48 Cal. St.B.J. 152 (1973); DeMeo Case Control III; *Litigation and Probate Charts*, 48 Cal.St.B.J. 410 (1973); Davis, *Docket Control and Law Office Filing Systems That Work In a Small Firm*, Ill. B.J. 360 (1972); Davis, *Docket Control and Filing Systems for the Small Law Firm*, 17 Prac. Law 35 (1971); Cantor, *Case Control*, 5 L. Off. Econ. & Man. 235 (1964); Perkin, *Time Management Without Pain*, 4 Lawyer's Day System 295 (1963).

charge of the system, and a procedure must be available to determine how it is to be handled. A procedure of requiring written approval to continue handling the matter has been implemented in several firms. A more drastic measure is to tie compliance to a partner's draw account. In the few instances where this procedure was adopted, compliance with the system, not surprisingly, was so consistent that the "punishment" aspect has not been utilized.

Fifth, the firm must insist that attorneys maintain individual calendars. A centralized system for control of pleadings, documents and anticipated action does not eliminate the responsibility of each attorney to calendar these events. An attorney's calendar should permit multiple entries on each day and should also disclose at least a one-week period of time on a single page. A calendar which does not permit legible entries for all significant due dates or which obscures the next day's material has obvious deficiencies which should not be accepted.

B. Differences Between Conflict of Interests and Calendar Systems

The approach to the calendar system is similar to the approach set forth for the conflict of interests system. Nonetheless, there are some differences which must be considered.

Instead of receiving all or most of the information at the initial interview (See Figure 3 again), the firm and responsible attorney will gather calendar information during the entire representation. Much of the data may come from some source other than the client, e.g., statute, court rule, opposing counsel, or various persons within the firm. A firm may include in its calendar system some or all of the following: appointments, corporate client securities reporting and tax filing dates, probate dates, filing and hearing dates, all litigation and court dates, follow-up dates, billing dates, professional (seminar) dates, and social commitments.

The update function within the calendar system also differs from the conflict of interests system. The information within the calendar system (the calendar information base) is frequently being changed. Dates are constantly added to an attorney's calendar, descriptions of matters to be completed and dates change regularly, and items are concluded frequently. The information collection process for the calendar information base is, almost always, client independent. That is, the client directly provides few of the work items or time deadlines. Thus, compared to the information base in the conflict of interests system, the firm has better control of information being introduced (input) to the calendar information base, but with the concomitant increase in responsibility.

The system must notify the attorney(s) or person(s) within the firm responsible for a work item in advance of the due date for the work item. The simplest system would be an index card system similar to the conflict system. The key would be the date the particular work item is due. The index card would contain the people to be notified of the activity to be performed. See Figure 7.

There are several variations on this theme. A typical one is called a perpetual calendar system. The index cards are moved or pulled as time goes on with new information being added to the file continually or perpetually. See Figure 8. Other variations include docket sheets, either in a separate notebook or as part of the client file. The index also may contain the client name and number, matter number and description, where the work item is to be performed, and opposing counsel. The additional information on the index cards permit a more complete search and more accurate calendaring. This advantage must be balanced with the increased effort to put the information on each notice. See Figure 9.

Collections of calendar information can provide other useful reports in addition to a reminder notice of a due date. The calendar information base also can generate reports keyed to the responsible attorney, the assigned attorney or paralegal, as well as a report for all matters involving a particular client.

Just as there were two methods to get multiple reports (reports using different keys) in the conflict of interests system, this can also be accomplished in the calendar system. The first method uses only one file and requires a review of each card in the one key (date) file. The individual must note all occurrences of the desired key (name), e.g., responsible attorney. The other method (and the more efficient and accurate one) entails duplicating each card as many times as there are keys. This duplication creates inverted files, exactly as described for the conflict of interests system. Only the information changes for the calendar information base, the theory is the same. For example, in the duplicate card calendar information base, for one calendared work item there would be an index card for the key-date, another (duplicate) card for the key-responsible attorney, another (duplicate) for the key-assigned attorney and paralegal, etc. See Figure 8.

The last area where the calendar system differs from the conflict of interests system is in the procedure used to cross-check and follow-up reported information. By use of the inverted index type of reporting, cross-checks are automatic. All items requiring attention will appear on at least two reports, and probably on more than two. The follow-up procedure can be accomplished by the individual who generates the reminder with the entry of another reminder. The dual reminder system is usually sufficient but a firm can modify the system to fit particular needs. See Figure 10. Aspects of the system, such as size and color of the reminders, should be determined by each firm.

The calendar information base will contain far more discrete items than the conflict of interests information base, and will receive a much higher degree of use. Because of the greater inquiry and because of the repetitive use of the data, the introduction of a machine will assist in achieving efficiency, accuracy and speed.

C. Information Gathering

Two characteristics which must be present to ensure the success of a calendar system information flow are full cooperation by those who gather the information *and* a defined calendar information collection procedure. There are basically two ways to ensure proper information gathering for the calendar system. Although many firms can envision or suggest other methods, the myriad of alternatives fall within one of the two basic classifications. One procedure is to initially forward documents to a calendar control department. The other procedure is to have individual attorneys control information gathering.

The latter method requires actual entry of the needed information into the system by the attorney, either by completing forms or using a terminal connected to the firm's computer. The central calendar department procedure requires the personnel in the calendar control department to review all pleadings and correspondence and, after categorizing and inputting the information, to forward the documents to the proper destination within the firm. The attorney-controlled procedure requires attorneys to note all commitments and utilize a control department only to file correspondence and enter information in the system.

Both information gathering techniques have drawbacks and advantages. The centralized method ensures consistent and rapid entry of the information, but it fails to provide needed attorney comments, delays information reaching attorneys, and provides little privacy to the individual attorney. On the other hand, allowing the attorney to input his own calendar information causes inconsistent input, requires education of many people on the detailed use of the system, and lacks adequate supervision. Combining the two methods cannot eliminate all deficiencies in either method but when the adopted method is tailored to the specific needs of a firm a reliable and efficient calendar system can be developed. No one system will apply to all firms given the different needs of firms and the equally different personalities of the various members of a firm.

Whether the information is gathered by form or computer terminal, by each attorney or a centralized department, a calendar information base must be updated with new information. If a terminal is used, the same form would appear before the operator on the display screen. The data is then entered and loaded into the information base. With a computer based system, the operator/clerk uses the programmed software, and electronically updates the calendar information base. On a manual system, the operator/clerk creates new index cards and places them in the file drawer.

D. Information Flow

To be most useful, the calendar system must have periodic reports, at least weekly, and preferably daily, setting out the commitments of the firm. The calendar report is constantly being changed and, therefore, biweekly or monthly reports become useless well before the new report is printed. By its very nature, updating the calendar information base causes the frequent generation of new reports. If a manual system, such as a basic card index system, is utilized, generating reports will consume a significant amount of time, especially in larger firms. However, manual systems are cost effective for smaller firms.

The computer, whether it is a word processor, an in-house computer, or a large service center, can make calendar control relatively inexpensive and manageable, especially in larger firms. As was shown with the conflict of interests system, the introduction of the machine does not change the logical flow of information and reporting. The machine is simply an additional resource to be used by the person(s) responsible for the firm's central calendar.

The use of a machine allows a large inverted file to be utilized with many more keys. A sampling of the information contained within a calendar information base and retrievable on each item (each item becomes a key) is as follows: date the work item is to be performed, attorney responsible for the matter, attorney or paralegal assigned to the work item, client name and number, matter number and description, opposing firm and attorneys, judge, court, court file number, caption, address of performance for work item, and narrative description of work item.

The procedure or flow of information in the calendar system is, in a practical sense, more complex than the conflict of interests system. Dates for commitments can be originated from within the firm by attorneys or paralegals, from pleadings or correspondence generated outside the firm, from statutory mandate (e.g., statute of limitations), from court rules and from an endless variety of agreed-upon due dates. Several people within the firm will want to review any given calendar item: the originating attorney, so that he can communicate effectively with his client; the responsible attorney, so he can allocate resources and supervise the work being performed; and the assigned individual, so that the work item can be completed. The variations are numerous, but each provides valuable information and cross-checks.

E. Utilizing Information

The individuals in the firm can now use the calendar information base to generate reports. The most typical report is one of all activities in the firm by date. A second report is a history-type report by matter, so that an individual looking at the matter file could see what has happened in the file (similar to a court docket sheet). In the actual processing of the calendar information and the physical act of transferring the information to a paper report in a readable and useable format, one can appreciate the real efficiencies of computers. With only a few keystrokes on a terminal, the computer (depending on the sophistication of the particular machine) can generate many reports in minutes. The depth of the report can be seen by listing some of the possible outputs:

1. Daily calendar - firm; a listing of all future and present activities showing all work items to be performed on each particular day;

2. Daily calendar - assigned attorney/paralegal; a listing for each assigned individual in the firm showing for that person the work items to be completed;

3. Weekly calendar - firm; same as daily calendar except showing a week in advance;

4. Weekly calendar - assigned attorney/paralegal; same as daily calendar except showing a week in advance;

5. Weekly calendar - responsible attorney; same as weekly calendar for assigned attorney but grouping all work items under the responsible attorney; and

6. Monthly calendar - matter; same as previous reports but listed and sorted by matter.

It is easy to develop 20 or more reports which incorporate various calendared items and provide numerous cross-checks for supervision and error prevention.

F.   Combining Systems

As the calendar system was described, it should be apparent that not only are the procedures the same or similar to those employed in the conflict of interests system, but some of the information is the same or similar. Although manual systems in these two areas are not manifestly economic to combine, computer-based systems are. The speed, size, storage capacity, and programs are just a few of the items which must be correlated before combining systems can guarantee time and money savings.

There are vast amounts of literature (propaganda) available on the equipment. The basic "entry" level equipment in the combined systems area is word processing equipment. There are dozens of manufacturers and vendors. See Figure 11. The capabilities and sophistication of these machines vary from rapid typewriters to complex hardware which can combine word processing with the conflict of interests and calendar information systems. The latter, referred to as data processing computers, add considerable capabilities. See Figure 12.

G. Other Equipment

Equipment does not end with the selection of the computer. Terminals, storage devices, data entry equipment, printers and telecommunication equipment must also be considered. The discussion of equipment is not meant to cause apprehension or anxiety in considering computer-based systems. However, the selection of equipment is not easy and necessitates balancing demands for speed and accuracy against available resources.

Computers (hardware) require personnel to program them before installation and to run them afterward. In order to function, all computers must have programs, usually referred to as software. Software is normally machine dependent and not all hardware and software are compatible. Most vendors of hardware provide a list of compatible software available through the vendor and other software companies. In addition, one may find the perfect conflict of interests system at one vendor, the perfect calendar system at another vendor, and the right machine at yet a third vendor.

Different computers and software require different levels of sophistication in operational personnel. A firm's decision on procedures within a system (computer or manual) also dictates different levels of skill. For instance, the operator/clerk who merely generates reports in the decentralized calendar system requires less education and training than the operator/clerk in the centralized calendar system. In the centralized system, the operator/clerk must review documents, identify dates and interpret court rules.

H. Conclusion

The successful system, whether it is a conflict of interests or calendar system, manual or computer system, must have five elements:

1. The responsibility for the supervision must be specifically assigned, usually to only one person. Security and errorless operation are directly related to controlled access;

2. The actual duties cannot be effectively performed by one person, thus proper and explicit delegation of duties is imperative;

3. All procedures and duties must be written. Oral and implied rules do not work;

4. The firm must require discipline by all members and employees, not just those few charged with specific duties. If individuals do not cooperate, any system will fail; and

5. The firm must provide the proper support to those charged with defining the firm's needs and directions, to those charged with buying equipment and programs, and to those who must perform the day-to-day work.

FIGURE 1.

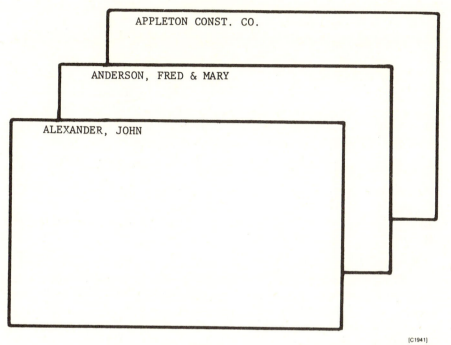

APPLETON CONST. CO.

ANDERSON, FRED & MARY

ALEXANDER, JOHN

[C1941]

FIGURE 2.

CLIENT: APPLETON CONST. CO. Date Opened: 6-24-78

CLIENT: ANDERSON, FRED & MARY Date Opened 1-18-79

CLIENT: ALEXANDER, JOHN   Date Opened: 1-1-80
ADDRESS: 111 Anyway   CL. NUMBER: 1234
      City, State 11111   MAT.NUMBER: ABC

MATTER: Tax Advice and Petition

CAPTION: Alexander v. U. S. A.

OPPOSING PARTY: USA

OPPOSING ATTORNEY: JOHN DOE

RESPONSIBLE ATTORNEY: FRED FLIM

ASSIGNED ATTORNEY: JACK FLAM

[C1942]

FIGURE 3.a

NEW BUSINESS MEMORANDUM

FOR RECORDS CENTER USE ONLY

CLIENT
MATTER
RECORDS _____
COMPUTER _____

SECTION 1. CLIENT/MATTER INFORMATION

CHECK APPROPRIATE BOX

☐ NEW CLIENT

☐ PRESENT CLIENT — NEW MATTER

☐ CLIENT NUMBER

CLIENT NAME / BILLING ADDRESS →

☐ CHANGE (TO FOLLOWING CLIENT/MATTER)

☐ CLIENT NUMBER
☐ MATTER NUMBER

DESCRIBE CHANGE _____

CLIENT NAME

BILLING ADDRESS FOR THIS MATTER

ATTN:
STREET
ADDRESS
CITY/STATE
ZIP
TELEPHONE ( )
CONTACT PERSON _____

SUGGEST MTTR NAME

DESCRIPTION OF WORK _____

	Number	Initials			
BILLING ATTY			☐ / ☐ / ☐	☐ TYPE OF LAW	☐ STATUTE OF LIMITATIONS _____
RESPONSIBLE ATTY			/ DATE OPENED		
ASSIGNED ATTY				☐ OFFICE (SF/LA)	☐ NO STATUTE OF LIMITATIONS

SECTION 2. FEE ARRANGEMENT

DEPT. HEAD APPROVAL (IF OTHER THAN HOURLY)

HOURLY	☐ H	
FIXED FEE	☐ F	_____
CONTINGENCY	☐ C	_____
RETAINER	☐ R	_____
NON-CHARGEABLE	☐ N	_____

RETAINER	☐ R	COST
NON-RETAINER	☐ N	CENTER
CUSTOMER PAYS FEE	☐ O	
EXECUTIVE SERVICES	☐ A	SPECIAL CODE
ACQUISITIONS/PUB. OFFERINGS	☐ X	(DO NOT USE)

SECTION 3. BILLING PROCEDURE

D N H V
BILLING FORMAT ☐ ☐ ☐ ☐   DEPT. HEAD APPROVAL IF FORMAT H OR V _____

M Q S A D
BILLING CYCLE ☐ ☐ ☐ ☐ ☐   DEPT. HEAD APPROVAL IF OTHER THAN M _____

FISCAL CODE ☐ FIRST MONTH OF BILLING CYCLE, IF NOT MONTHLY   REMINDER STATEMENTS ☐ YES ☐ NO

SECTION 4. FIRM ADMINISTRATION

COMPLETED BY ATTORNEY/SECRETARY

OPENED BY	_____
TYPE OF FILE	_____
DELIVER FILE TO	_____
SOURCE OF BUSINESS	_____

COMPLETED BY RECORDS CENTER ONLY

FILE CHANGE ACTION	_____
CONFLICT CHECK	_____
SOURCE OF BUSINESS CODE	☐☐☐☐☐

SECTION 5. PARTIES TO TRANSACTIONS (INCLUDING CONFLICTS)

PARTY   *RELATIONSHIP TO ABOVE CLIENT*

1 _____   1 _____
2 _____   2 _____
3 _____   3 _____
4 _____   4 _____

ENCLOSE CONTINUATION SHEET FOR LITIGATION MATTERS OR ADDITIONAL PARTIES

SECTION 6. COMMENTS

[C2004]

FIGURE 3.b

JONES & SMITH

NEW CLIENT INFORMATION   (TO BE COMPLETED FOR NEW CLIENTS ONLY)

DATE FILE OPENED _____

NAME (30) _____

ADDRESS _____   ORIGINATING ATTORNEY _____
(30 each line)   (INITIALS)

_____   CLIENT GROUP NUMBER _____

_____   NEW BUSINESS CREDIT _____
                                                                                                          (YES/NO)

_____

NEW MATTER INFORMATION   (TO BE COMPLETED FOR ALL NEW MATTER)

CLIENT NUMBER _____ CLIENT NAME _____

MATTER NAME   (35) _____

NATURE OF MATTER _____

AREA OF LAW _____ CLIENT'S REFERENCE NUMBER (12) _____

FEE BASIS (8) NORMAL HOURLY RATE _____ _____ _____ . _____ _____ _____ (9) AGREED FEE $ _____
                                                         A   B   C   D   E   F

(10) CONTINGENT FEE% _____(12) TO BE DETERMINED BY ALL RELEVANT FACTORS _____

(11) SPECIAL HOURLY RATES

              PARTNERS $ _____ (13) TO BE ALLOWED BY COURT_____

              ASSOCIATES $ _____ (14) RETAINER   _____

              LEGAL ASSISTANTS $ _____ ESTIMATE GIVEN TO CLIENT $ _____

BILLING FREQUENCY MONTHLY _____ QUARTERLY _____COMPLETION _____

BILLING ATTORNEY _____RESPONSIBLE ATTORNEY_____

ASSIGNED ATTORNEYS/LEGAL ASSISTANTS   #1 _____ #2 _____ #3 _____ #4 _____

NAMES TO BE CROSSED INDEXED (FOR POSSIBLE CONFLICTS)_____

_____   _____

_____   _____

DOCKET _____ _____ACCEPTANCE OF EMPLOYMENT ORIGINATED BY ASSOCIATE APPROVED BY (PARTNER)_____
              YES   NO

HOW CLIENT CAME TO FIRM_____
REMARKS (INCLUDING ADDRESS TO BE USED FOR BILLING IF DIFFERENT THAN CLIENT ADDRESS)

_____
_____
_____
_____

SECRETARY _____
                  (INITIALS)

[C1943]

FIGURE 3.c

NEW MATTER REPORT

CLIENT INFORMATION

CLIENT: _____

ADDRESS: _____

(City)   (Code)

BUSINESS PHONE: _____

CONTACT: _____ HOME PHONE: _____

Date _____ 19 ____

⬭ NEW CLIENT

⬭ PRESENT CLIENT

CLIENT NUMBER _____

MATTER INFORMATION

FILE NAME: _____

NATURE OF MATTER: _____

_____

_____

_____

AMOUNT INVOLVED: _____ AREA OF PRACTICE CODE: _____

OPPOSING PARTY: _____

     Name   Address   Phone No.

OPPOSING LAWYER: _____

     Name   Address   Phone No.

FEE ARRANGEMENT

⬭ FIXED FEE OF $ _____ OR RANGE OF $ _____ TO $ _____

⬭ TIME RATE _____

⬭ CONTINGENCY OF: _____

⬭ FEE TO BE DETERMINED ON BASIS OF WORK DONE, TAKING INTO ACCOUNT ALL RELEVANT FACTORS.

⬭ OTHER: _____

ESTIMATED FEE $ _____

BILLING PROCEDURE

⬭ NEW GENERAL RETAINER $ _____ PER _____ EFFECTIVE _____

⬭ OPENING ADVANCE OF $ _____

⬭ BILLING INSTRUCTIONS FOR BOOKKEEPER:

	MONTHLY	QUARTERLY	UPON CONCLUSION	OTHER
FEE	⬭	⬭	⬭	⬭
DISBURSEMENTS	⬭	⬭	⬭	⬭

OTHER: _____

FILES

FILE CARDS PREPARED BY: _____ DATE _____

⬭ OPEN NEW FILE   ⬭ INCLUDE IN EXISTING FILE   ⬭ NO FILE

FILES CHECKED FOR CONFLICT OF INTEREST BY: _____ DATE _____

FIRM ADMINISTRATION

OPENED BY _____

ENGAGEMENT RECEIVED FROM _____

RESPONSIBLE LAWYER _____

ENGAGEMENT RECEIVED BY _____

ASSIGNED LAWYERS _____

COMMENTS _____

REMARKS

_____

_____

_____

_____

FIGURE 4.a

HOW TO USE THIS FORM: The white card is your active client index. File under the client's name. The blue card is your adverse party index. File under the adverse party name in a separate index tray. The buff copy is gummed and perforated. Use the top part as a file label and the lower part to head your accounting ledger - or paste the copy into the file folder for reference.

Type client name in CAPS, adverse party in lower case. When the file closes, complete the white card and file in the closed client index. Use the blue card to calendar destruction.

Client		Adverse Party	File No.
Address			Phones
Matter			Date Opened / Attorney Handling
Insurer/ Forwarder			
Opposing Counsel			
Cross Index Names			
Memo			
Closed Date	Destroy Date		Closed Number
Client		Adverse Party	File No.

[C1945]

FIGURE 4.b

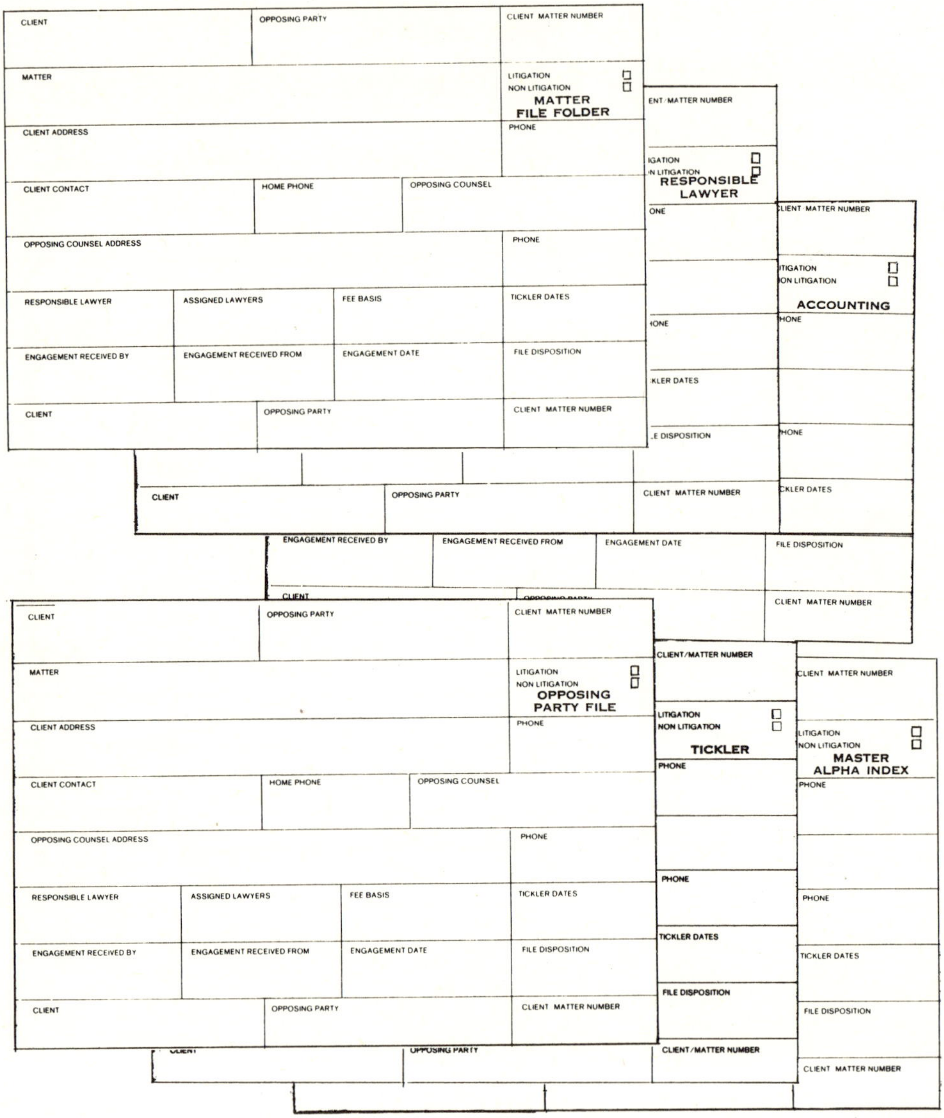

[C 1946]

FIGURE 4.c.1

CONFLICT FILE

<u>KEY</u> FILE <u>CLIENT</u>

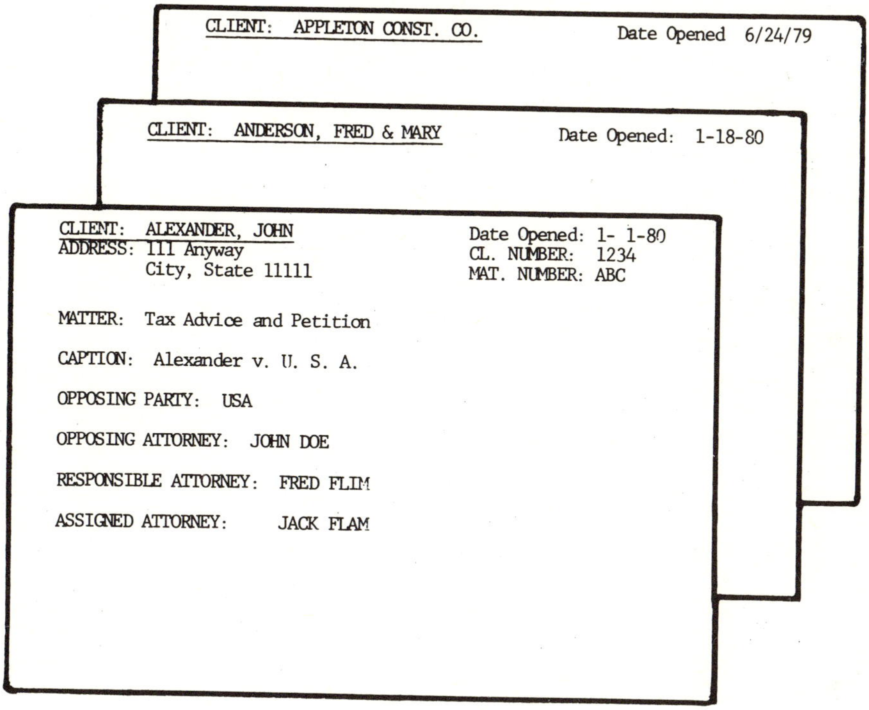

<u>CLIENT:</u> APPLETON CONST. CO.   Date Opened 6/24/79

<u>CLIENT:</u> ANDERSON, FRED & MARY   Date Opened: 1-18-80

<u>CLIENT:</u> <u>ALEXANDER, JOHN</u>   Date Opened: 1- 1-80
<u>ADDRESS:</u> <u>111 Anyway</u>   CL. NUMBER: 1234
         City, State 11111   MAT. NUMBER: ABC

MATTER: Tax Advice and Petition

CAPTION: Alexander v. U. S. A.

OPPOSING PARTY: USA

OPPOSING ATTORNEY: JOHN DOE

RESPONSIBLE ATTORNEY: FRED FLIM

ASSIGNED ATTORNEY: JACK FLAM

[C1947]

FIGURE 4.c.2

CONFLICT FILE

<u>KEY FILE DATE</u>

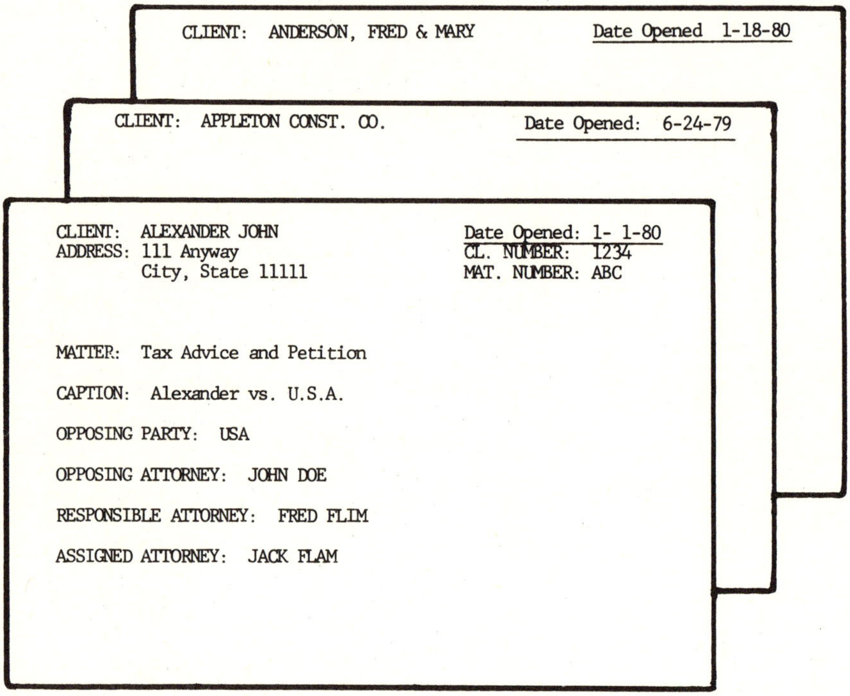

CLIENT: ANDERSON, FRED & MARY   <u>Date Opened 1-18-80</u>

CLIENT: APPLETON CONST. CO.   <u>Date Opened: 6-24-79</u>

```
CLIENT:   ALEXANDER JOHN          Date Opened: 1- 1-80
ADDRESS: 111 Anyway              CL. NUMBER:  1234
         City, State 11111       MAT. NUMBER: ABC


MATTER:  Tax Advice and Petition

CAPTION:  Alexander vs. U.S.A.

OPPOSING PARTY:  USA

OPPOSING ATTORNEY:   JOHN DOE

RESPONSIBLE ATTORNEY:   FRED FLIM

ASSIGNED ATTORNEY:   JACK FLAM
```

[C1948]

FIGURE 4.c.3

CONFLICT FILE

KEY FILE RESPONSIBLE ATTORNEY

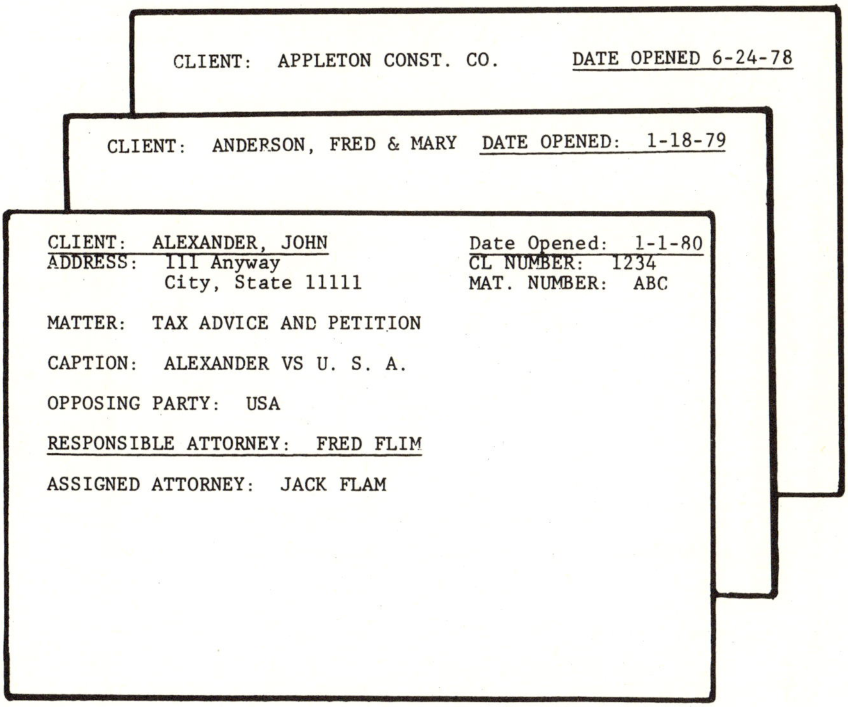

```
CLIENT:  APPLETON CONST. CO.          DATE OPENED 6-24-78

   CLIENT:  ANDERSON, FRED & MARY    DATE OPENED:  1-18-79

CLIENT:   ALEXANDER, JOHN            Date Opened:   1-1-80
ADDRESS:   111 Anyway                CL NUMBER:   1234
           City, State 11111         MAT. NUMBER:   ABC

MATTER:   TAX ADVICE AND PETITION

CAPTION:   ALEXANDER VS U. S. A.

OPPOSING PARTY:   USA

RESPONSIBLE ATTORNEY:   FRED FLIM

ASSIGNED ATTORNEY:   JACK FLAM
```

[C1949]

FIGURE 5

REPORT ON POTENTIALLY
ADVERSE CLIENT RELATIONSHIPS

DATE: 1/2/80
PAGE: 1 of 1

CLIENT BEING REVIEWED

CLIENT NAME	CLIENT NUMBER	MATTER NUMBER	DATE EMPLOYED	CLIENT POSITION	CAPTION
Corp., Inc.	1234	5678	12/15/79	Plaintiff	Corp., Inc. v. Big Computer Co., Inc.

INDUSTRY	DESCRIPTION OF MATTER	TYPE OF MATTER
Computers	Civil antitrust action by client seeking treble damages	Antitrust Litigation

ATTORNEYS	OTHER PARTIES AFFILIATES	CLIENT AFFILIATES
Joseph Justice	Small Computer Co., Inc. (Big Computer Co., Inc.)	Tiny Computer Co., Inc.

POTENTIALLY ADVERSE RELATIONSHIPS

1. CLIENT NAME	CLIENT NUMBER	MATTER NUMBER	DATE EMPLOYED	CLIENT POSITION	CAPTION
Small Computer Co., Inc.	0123	0321	4/23/75	Defendant	Smith v. Small Computer Co., Inc.

INDUSTRY	DESCRIPTION OF MATTER	TYPE OF MATTER	MATTER STATUS
Computers	Age discrimination suit by employee	Individual rights Litigation	Closed 2/15/77

2. CLIENT NAME	CLIENT NUMBER	MATTER NUMBER	DATE EMPLOYED	CLIENT POSITION	CAPTION
Jane Jones	0234	0432	6/6/77	Plaintiff	Jones v. Tiny Computer Co., Inc.

INDUSTRY	DESCRIPTION OF MATTER	TYPE OF MATTER	MATTER STATUS
Computers	Breach of contract by D for consulting services by P	Contracts	Open

[C2123]

FIGURE 6
CONFLICT

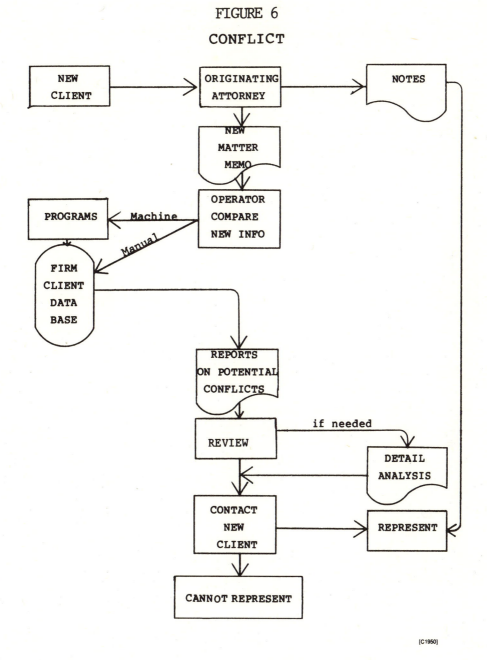

[C1950]

FIGURE 7.a

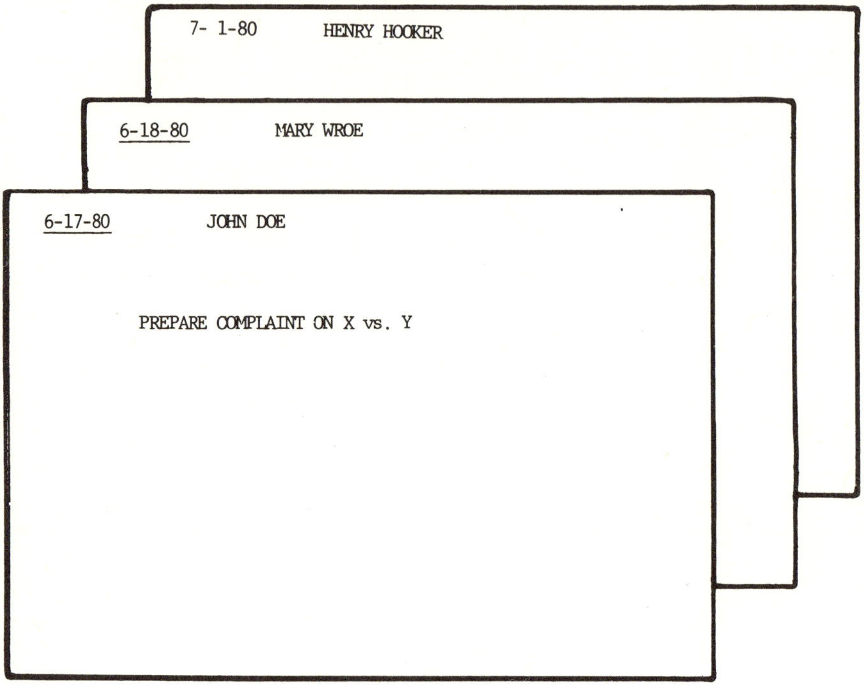

```
7- 1-80        HENRY HOOKER

    6-18-80         MARY WROE

  6-17-80          JOHN DOE


     PREPARE COMPLAINT ON X vs. Y
```

[C1951]

FIGURE   7.b

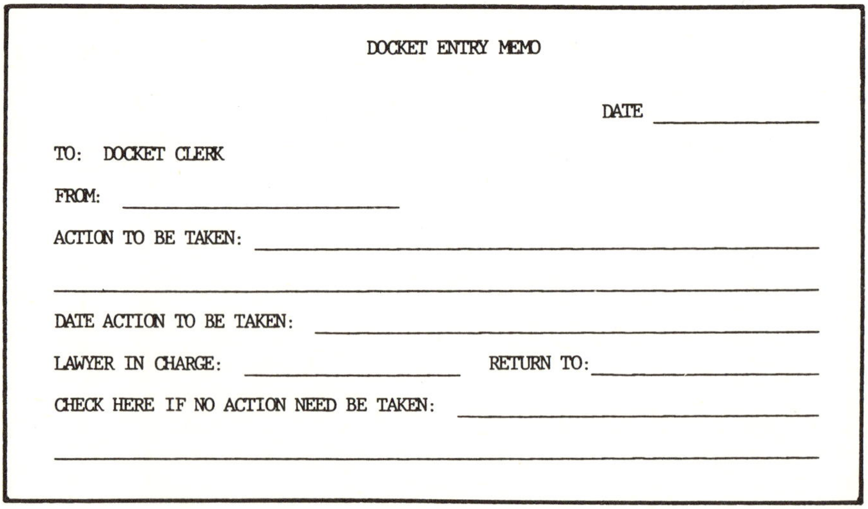

```
                    DOCKET ENTRY MEMO

                                    DATE _____

TO:  DOCKET CLERK
FROM:  _____
ACTION TO BE TAKEN:  _____
_____
DATE ACTION TO BE TAKEN:  _____
LAWYER IN CHARGE:  _____   RETURN TO:_____
CHECK HERE IF NO ACTION NEED BE TAKEN:  _____
_____
```

[C1952]

FIGURE 7.c

NOTIFICATION OF ACTION TAKEN

TO: DOCKET CLERK

FROM:

CASE: _____

DATE ACTION TO BE TAKEN: _____

ACTION REQUIRED: _____

_____

_____

DATE OF COMPLETION: _____

[C1953]

FIGURE 8.a

DATE KEY FILE

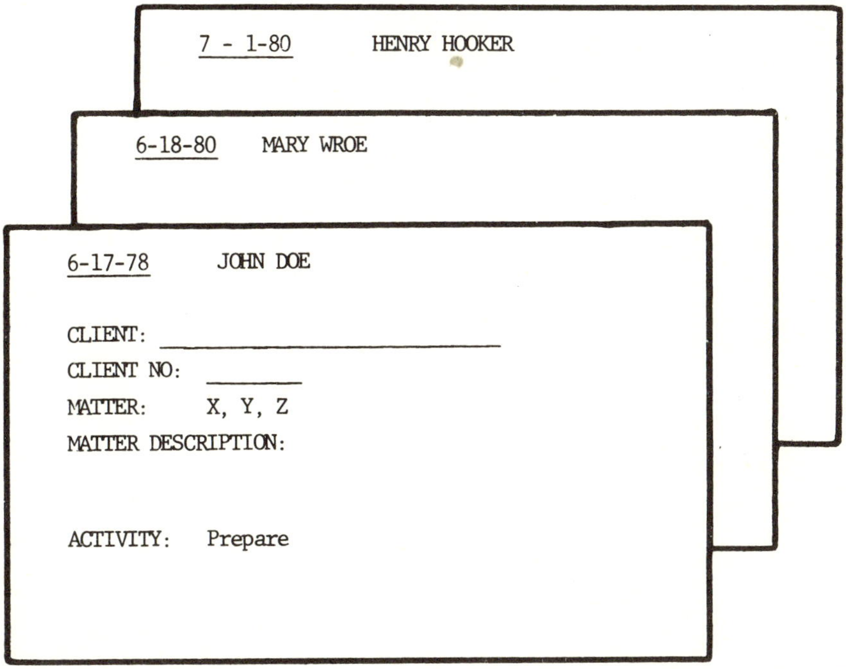

7 - 1-80   HENRY HOOKER

6-18-80   MARY WROE

6-17-78   JOHN DOE

CLIENT: _____

CLIENT NO: _____

MATTER: X, Y, Z

MATTER DESCRIPTION:

ACTIVITY: Prepare

[C1954]

FIGURE 8.b
NAME KEY FILE

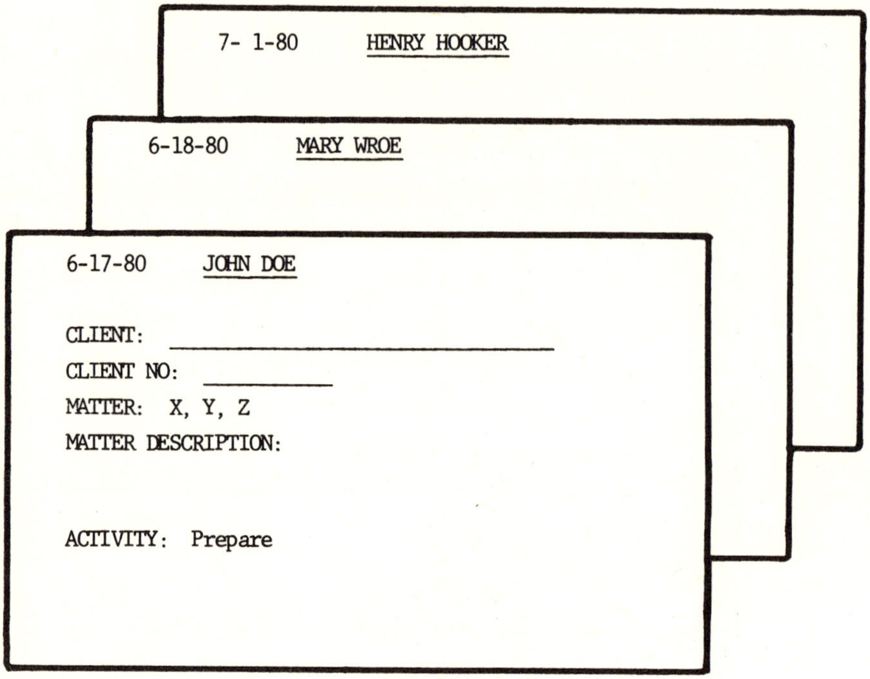

```
                7- 1-80      HENRY HOOKER
          6-18-80      MARY WROE
    6-17-80     JOHN DOE

    CLIENT:  _____

    CLIENT NO:  _____
    MATTER:  X, Y, Z
    MATTER DESCRIPTION:


    ACTIVITY:  Prepare
```

[C1955]

FIGURE 9.a

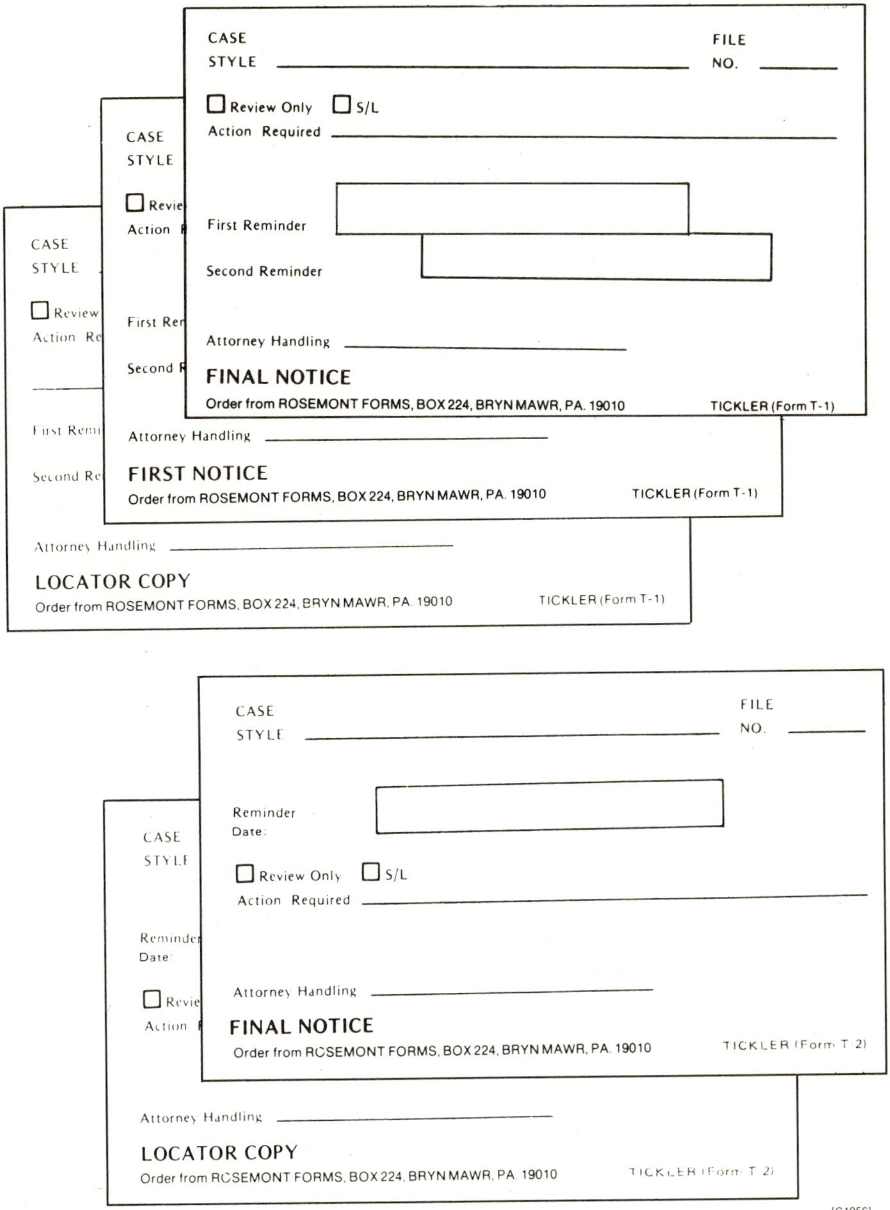

CASE
STYLE _____ FILE
NO. _____

☐ Review Only ☐ S/L
Action Required _____

First Reminder

Second Reminder

Attorney Handling _____

FINAL NOTICE
Order from ROSEMONT FORMS, BOX 224, BRYN MAWR, PA. 19010   TICKLER (Form T-1)

CASE
STYLE _____

☐ Revie
Action F

First Rer

Second F

Attorney Handling _____

FIRST NOTICE
Order from ROSEMONT FORMS, BOX 224, BRYN MAWR, PA. 19010   TICKLER (Form T-1)

CASE
STYLE _____

☐ Review
Action Re

First Remi

Second Re

Attorney Handling _____

LOCATOR COPY
Order from ROSEMONT FORMS, BOX 224, BRYN MAWR, PA. 19010   TICKLER (Form T-1)

CASE
STYLE _____ FILE
NO. _____

Reminder
Date:

☐ Review Only ☐ S/L
Action Required _____

Attorney Handling _____

FINAL NOTICE
Order from ROSEMONT FORMS, BOX 224, BRYN MAWR, PA. 19010   TICKLER (Form T-2)

CASE
STYLE

Reminder
Date:

☐ Revie
Action F

Attorney Handling _____

LOCATOR COPY
Order from ROSEMONT FORMS, BOX 224, BRYN MAWR, PA. 19010   TICKLER (Form T-2)

[C 1956]

FIGURE 9.b

REMINDER DATE Month __March__ Day __10__ Year __1980__
DUE DATE Mo. __April__ Day __15__ Year __1980__ Time __9:30__

REMINDER DATE Month __March__ Day __10__ Year __1980__
DUE DATE Mo. __April__ Day __15__ Year __1980__ Time __9:30__

REMINDER DATE Month __March__ Day __10__ Year __1980__
DUE DATE Mo. __April__ Day __15__ Year __1980__ Time __9:30__
Client/Matter __Jones v. Smith, Contract__ File No. __124-1__
To Lawyer(s) __LDH, HWZ__
Note(s) __Prepare to present claim under contract__
__for review by Smithand counsel__

Statute of Limitations Date _____   Completed ☐   Reschedule To _____
Entered By _____ Date _____

IMPORTANT REMINDER/ASSIGNMENT

© 1978 Safeguard Business Systems, Inc.

[C1957]

FIGURE 10.a

ATTORNEY CALENDAR MONITOR
REPORT FOR PERIOD
1/8/80 to 1/12/80

1/5/80
PAGE 1 of 1

ATTORNEY

JOSEPH JUSTICE

1.
DATE ACTION REQUIRED	CLIENT NUMBER	MATTER NUMBER	CLIENT NAME	CASE CAPTION
1/8/80	3210	7654	I.M. Sued	John Doe v. I.M. Sued

ACTION REQUIRED: Answer to complaint due in superior court.

ACTION TAKEN: _____   DATE ACTION TAKEN / /

NEXT ACTION REQUIRED: _____   DATE ACTION REQUIRED / /

2.
DATE ACTION REQUIRED	CLIENT NUMBER	MATTER NUMBER	CLIENT NAME	CASE CAPTION
1/10/80	1234	5678	Corp, Inc.	Corp, Inc. v. Big Computer Co., Inc.

ACTION REQUIRED: Report due on potentially adverse client relationships

ACTION TAKEN: _____   DATE ACTION TAKEN / /

NEXT ACTION REQUIRED: _____   DATE ACTION REQUIRED / /

[C1958]

FIGURE 10.b

CLIENT CALENDAR MONITOR   1/5/80
REPORT FOR PERIOD   PAGE 1 of 1

1/8/80 to 1/12/80

CLIENT NAME	CLIENT NUMBER				
Corp, Inc.	1234				

	MATTER NUMBER	CASE CAPTION	ATTORNEYS	DATE ACTION REQUIRED	ACTION REQUIRED
1.	5678	Corp, Inc. V.	Joseph Justice	1/10/80	Report due on potentially adverse client relationships.
2.	6789	Keying Co. V. Corp, Inc.	Jane Doe	1/11/80	Deposition of client vice president by plaintiff.

(C 1959)

FIGURE 10.c

MATTER CALENDAR MONITOR   1/5/80
REPORT FOR PERIOD   PAGE 1 of 1

1/8/80 to 1/12/80

MATTER NUMBER	CLIENT NUMBER	CLIENT NAME	CASE CAPTION	ATTORNEYS
7654	3210	I. M. Sued	John Doe v. I. M. Sued	Joseph Justice

DATE ACTION REQUIRED	ACTION REQUIRED
1. 1/8/80	Answer to complaint due in Superior Court.

(C 1960)

FIGURE 10.d

REPORT ON MATTERS INACTIVE   1/5/80
FOR PAST 30, 60 OR 90-PLUS DAYS   PAGE 1 of 1

1/8/80 to 1/12/80

MATTERS INACTIVE FOR PAST 30 DAYS

	CLIENT NUMBER	MATTER NUMBER	CLIENT NAME	CASE CAPTION	ATTORNEYS	DATE OF LAST ACTION	DESCRIPTION OF LAST ACTION TAKEN
1.	1111	2222	Jane Smith	Jane Smith V. John Smith	Joseph Justice	12/1/79	Settlement offer made by client

MATTERS INACTIVE FOR PAST 90-PLUS DAYS

	CLIENT NUMBER	MATTER NUMBER	CLIENT NAME	CASE CAPTION	ATTORNEYS	DATE OF LAST ACTION	DESCRIPTION OF LAST ACTION TAKEN
1.	3333	4444	ABC Co.	DEF Co. V. ABC Co.	Jane Doe	6/6/79	Oral argument in Court of Appeals

(C 1961)

FIGURE 11.

Word Processor

A. *Stand Alone*

  1. Exxon Qyx—level 1, 1A, 2, 3, 4

     Qyx Division

     Exxon Information Systems

     P. O. Box 1979

     Wayne, PA 19807

  2. Vydec, Inc.

     130 Algonquin Parkway

     Whippany, NY 07981

  3. Xerox 800, 850

     Xerox Square

     Rochester, NY 14644

  4. IBM OS6/420, 430, 440, 450, 452

     General Systems Division

     P. O. Box 2150

     Atlanta, GA 30301

  5. Wang WP5, WPS 20, 25, 30

     One Industrial Avenue

     Lowell, MA 01851

  6. NBI II 3000

     1695 38th Street

     P. O. Box 9001

     Boulder, CO 80301

  7. Lanier, No Problem II LC

     1700 Chantilly Drive, N.E.

     Atlanta, GA 30324

  8. CPT, 6000, 8000

     1001 Second Street South

     Hopkins, MN 55343

  9. AM Jacquard AM text, J500, 225

     1639 11th Street

     Santa Monica, CA 90404

  10. Olivetti, TES501, 701

     500 Park Avenue

     New York, NY 10022

11. Digital Equip. Corp (DEC) WPS 78
     Maynard, MA 01754

B. *Shared Logic*

1. Xerox, 800, 850, 860
    Xerox Square
    Rochester, NY 14644

2. IBM OS6/420, 430, 440, 450, 452, S/34
    General Systems Division
    P. O. Box 2150
    Atlanta, GA 30301

3. Wang, WPS 20, 25, 30, OIS 130, 140, 145, VS
    One Industrial Avenue
    Lowell, MA 01851

4. Lanier, No Problem, NP IILC, Wordplex
    1700 Chantilly Drive, N.E.
    Atlanta, GA 30324

5. Four Phase, Foreword
    10700 N. DeAnza Boulevard
    Cupertino, CA 95014

6. Kubernan
    Cloverdale Executive Bldg.
    2110 Cloverdale Avenue
    Winston-Salem, NC 27103

7. AM Jacquard AM text, J500, 225, 100, 105
    1639 11th Street
    Santa Monica, CA 90404

8. Mini Computer Systems, Factfinder
    525 Executive Boulevard
    Elmsford, NY 10523

9. Compute-R-Systems, CRS
    935 S. Trooper Road
    P. O. Box 267
    Norristown, PA 19404

10. Comptek Research (Barrister), 200, 220, 300

455 Cayuga Road

Buffalo, NY 14225

11. CompuTrac, Hewlett Packard

14200 Midway Road, Suite 100

Dallas, TX 75240

12. Digital Equip. Corp (DEC), WPS 78, WS 200, RSTS PDPII

Maynard, MA 01754

FIGURE 12.

Mini/Micro

1. Wang Laboratories, Inc.

One Industrial Avenue
Lowell, MA 01851

2. IBM

General Systems Division
P. O. Box 2150
Atlanta, GA 30301

3. Digital Equip. Corp.

Maynard, MA 01754

4. Four-Phase

10700 N. DeAnza Boulevard
Cupertino, CA 95014

5. Mini-Computer Systems (Factfinder)

525 Executive Boulevard
Elmsford, NY 10523

6. Data General

Southboro, MA 01772

7. Compute-R-Systems

935 S. Trooper Road
P. O. Box 267
Norristown, PA 19404

8. Comptek Research (Barrister)

455 Cayuga Road
Buffalo, NY 14225

Chapter 3
PREVENTING ERRORS IN SECURITIES TRANSACTIONS

Jeffrey M. Smith
and
William S. Jacobs

Section I
INTRODUCTION

While this Chapter is based on a concern for legal malpractice in the area of securities law, its focus is broader than traditional malpractice concepts in several respects. For this reason the word "errors" has been substituted for the word "malpractice" in the discussion which follows. This substitution reflects the authors' concern not merely with attorney liability arising from securities transactions, but also with preventing the misstatements, omissions or registration violations that may or may not result in actual liability, depending on the attorney's role and state of mind or level of care. As used herein, the term "errors" will refer to inadequate disclosure or other failure to satisfy applicable requirements or standards, regardless of whether they occur in circumstances rendering the attorney liable. Of course, some of the procedures discussed herein will assist, in varying degrees, in defending against liability in the event an error does occur by, for example, establishing that the attorney has met the applicable standard of care.

The use of the term "errors" also reflects that securities transactions involve broader potential for attorney liability than is usually implied by the use of the term "legal malpractice," that is, a breach of duty by an attorney to a client with whom the attorney had an express contract for performing legal services.[1] In addition to parties in privity of contract with an attorney, purchasers of securities, accountants and others may have a basis for pursuing an attorney for damages they have suffered in connection with a securities transaction. Furthermore, while other governmental agencies can also theoretically take action against attorneys, the Securities and Exchange Commission (SEC) has actively pursued such actions and has also pressured attorneys to aid the SEC in its law enforcement activities. The term "legal malpractice" is sometimes applicable in such actions, but often SEC actions do not raise issues customarily involved in more traditional legal malpractice cases.

---

1. *See* Mallen & Levit, Legal Malpractice
2–3 (West Publishing Co. 1977).

The primary purpose of this Chapter is to analyze policies and procedures that law firms can utilize to prevent errors that may lead to adversary proceedings against them, whether the claimant be the SEC or a member of the private sector,[2] and that will assist in the defense of such actions even if an error does occur. Although some of these policies and procedures will entail substantive legal considerations, the discussion here includes only a brief overview of the statutory and common-law bases for liability arising from securities transactions.

In addition, this Chapter is not intended even to attempt to instruct attorneys on how to properly complete registration forms or conduct a private placement. The policies and procedures discussed here are, however, intended to call attention to some significant pitfalls, and generally to assist an attorney in rendering legal services in the securities area in a manner that is less likely to involve errors, and that is more likely to survive the after-the-fact scrutiny of disgruntled investors and the SEC, whether or not errors do occur. Finally, the principal focus of this Chapter is securities transactions which involve raising capital to finance a business enterprise. This type of transaction, not more specialized matters such as proxy solicitations or broker-dealer regulation, is likely to arise in the practices of a broad spectrum of attorneys; also it is in the area of capital formation that most actions arise against attorneys for securities violations.

If every policy and procedure mentioned in this Chapter were adopted by a law firm and applied to every securities transaction it handled, their benefits to both the attorneys and clients would plainly be outweighed by the unnecessary delay and other problems created by such an across-the-board application. The authors' conception of these policies and procedures is that they constitute a checklist for use in evaluating the degree of protection against errors that a firm is building into a transaction, and for use in selecting policies and procedures that are appropriate in the circumstances of a particular transaction.

To some extent, certain of the policies and procedures may serve as substitutes for one another. For example, if a firm is not familiar with a client and its business, it would be appropriate to utilize more extensive inquiries to verify and support critical facts that the client presents to the firm. Similarly, if a firm does not implement a stringent policy regarding the transmission of information within the firm concerning mergers, takeovers, proxy fights, and related business and legal disputes, a more restrictive policy would be appropriate with respect to purchases and sales by attorneys of clients' securities. In any event, judgment and discretion are required.

On a related note, the policies and procedures discussed in this Chapter should not be considered a final product. Just as this Chapter was

2. While Disciplinary Rule 6–102(A) of the ABA Code of Professional Responsibility prohibits attorneys from limiting their liability to clients for errors, there is clearly no prohibition against preventing errors in the first instance.

developed in part from earlier treatments of the subject,[3] future developments in this area of law, further analysis by other writers, and the accumulated experience of accomplished securities practitioners with these and other policies and procedures, will undoubtedly expand, refine and improve the approaches discussed here. Nor should they be viewed as any effort on the part of the authors to establish either standards or generally accepted procedures for the practice of securities law, nor as an endorsement of SEC suggestions that attorneys have a duty to perform one or another role or procedure. In examining policies and procedures that are believed to reduce the exposure to error and liability in securities transactions, the authors are not suggesting that the risk of such exposure would be unacceptably high if a particular procedure was not used. In this sense, this Chapter deals in comparative exposure, not absolutes, and statements that a particular procedure "should" be followed are intended to be read as if prefaced by the phrase, "In order to reduce risk, ..."

Finally, as mentioned in Chapters 1 and 2, the term "conflict of interests" is utilized for ease of recognition. The ABA Code of Professional Responsibility includes that term in the definition of the broader term "differing interests." The authors' intention is that "conflict of interests" be read here as the equivalent of "differing interests."

Section II

UNCONTROLLABLE FACTORS

Over the last 15 years, litigation in general has sharply increased in this country. Between 1967 and 1976, there was an increase of 84% in the number of civil actions filed in the federal district courts.[4] Moreover, it has been estimated that if the growth rate in the number of appeals taken from district court decisions remains constant, the number of judges assigned to the various courts of appeals will increase by a factor of 50 by the year 2010.[5]

Actions against attorneys have also increased sharply.[6] The experience of St. Paul Fire and Marine Insurance Company, which historically was a leading insurer of attorneys, is illustrative. Between 1971 and 1975, the

3. The authors wish to acknowledge the significant contributions of Frank M. Wozencraft, *Policies and Procedures for Law Firms*, PLI Sixth Annual Institute on Securities Regulation 221 (1975), and of John C. Chappell and James H. Cheek III, *The Development of Law Firm Policies and Procedures Relating to Securities Matters*, PLI Ninth Annual Institute of Securities Regulation 639 (1977). In addition, this Chapter is also based on an article by Jeffrey M. Smith, *Preventing Errors In*

Securities Transactions, 30 S.Car.L. Rev. 243 (1979).

4. *The Chilling Impact of Litigation*, Bus. Week, June 6, 1977, at 58.

5. *Id.* (Estimate by Professor John Barton of Stanford Law School). The estimated increase was from the then existing number of approximately 100 appellate judges to 5,000 in the year 2010.

6. *See* Mallen & Levit, *supra* note 1, at 15–16.

number of new insureds increased by 34%, but this was accompanied by a 90% increase in the number of reported liability claims against new insureds.[7] The general increase in litigation, and at least a portion of the increase in litigation involving attorneys, is due in part to a significant increase over the last 10 years in the supply of two factors--attorneys and causes of action. Over 450,000 attorneys are now practicing in the United States, an increase of approximately 50% over the number of practicing attorneys 10 years ago. Society has apparently rejected Shakespeare's advice, "The first thing we do, let's kill all the lawyers."[8] We now have over 17 lawyers for every 10,000 people, which is approximately 2½ times the per capita rate in Great Britain, which not so many years ago was the source of a large portion of American legal principles and attitudes.[9]

Although no direct proof exists correlating the increase in the number of attorneys to the increase in litigation, including litigation against attorneys, it would seem that if the supply of attorneys were restricted the incidence of litigation would be reduced. Also, as the supply of attorneys in a given community increases, the percentage of attorneys with whom any one attorney is familiar decreases. It is obviously psychologically easier to engage in litigation against a relative stranger or mere acquaintance than a friend, and it becomes even easier if one has never met the defendant.

The increases in implied causes of action in the area of securities law,[10] and of asserted duties under the securities law, are also contributing factors to the exposure faced by attorneys who practice in this field. While the creativity of attorneys representing private parties in securities litigation has contributed to this increase, the SEC has also been a major force in this expansion. The change in its attitude towards various aspects of law over the last 15 years is perhaps best illustrated by a comparison of the following two administrative actions. In 1962, in *In re American Finance Co.*[11] the SEC stated:

> Though owing a public responsibility, an attorney in acting as the client's advisor, defender, advocate and confidant enters into a personal relationship in which his principal concern is with the interests and rights of his client. The requirement of the [1933] Act of certification by an independent accountant, on the other hand, is intended to secure for the benefit of public investors the detached objectivity of a disinterested person.[12]

7. Informational Report, ABA Special Committee on Lawyers' Professional Liability 4 (Feb. 1977).

8. King Henry VI, Part II, Act IV, scene ii, line 86.

9. *See generally* A. Kaufman, Problems in Professional Responsibility 9–12 (1976).

10. *See, e.g.,* J. I. Case Co. v. Borak, 377 U.S. 426 (1964) (proxy rules); Fisch-

man v. Raytheon Mfg. Co., 188 F.2d 783 (2d Cir. 1951) (§ 17 of the Securities Act of 1933); Kardon v. National Gypsum Co., 69 F.Supp. 512 (E.D. Pa. 1946) (Rule 10b–5).

11. 40 S.E.C. 1043, [1961–64 Transfer Binder] Fed. Sec. L. Rep. (CCH) ¶ 76,-832 (1962).

12. 40 S.E.C., at 1049.

By 1973, the SEC's approach had changed dramatically, as demonstrated by the following quotation from *In re Emanuel Fields:* [13]

> Members of this Commission have pointed out time and time again that the task of enforcing the securities laws rests in overwhelming measure on the bar's shoulders. These were statements of what all who are versed in the practicalities of securities law know to be a truism, *i.e.,* that this Commission with its small staff, limited resources, and onerous tasks is peculiarly dependent on the probity and the diligence of the professionals who practice before it . . .. This is a field where unscrupulous lawyers can inflict irreparable harm on those who rely on the disclosure document that they produce.

Also, in 1973 the SEC instituted its action against National Student Marketing Corp., its attorneys, and other individuals.[14] In 1977, this suit was settled by some, but not all, of the attorney-defendants in that action.[15] In 1978, the remaining attorney-defendants were found to have aided and abetted violations of the federal securities laws,[16] and later settled the matter after appellate briefs had been filed.

Demonstrating that litigation with clients is just as dangerous as adversary proceedings with the SEC, and that there can be substantial incentive for pursuing a potential cause of action, a jury in Denver recently returned a verdict of $2.2 million against attorneys in a malpractice case based on errors in a relatively basic securities transaction.[17] It was subsequently settled for $1.2 million.[18]

Finally, the basic attitude of people in the United States towards the legal profession cannot be ignored as a contributing factor to the problem of increased litigation against attorneys. In a 1976 Gallup Poll,[19] less than 25% of those responding rated the ethical standards and honesty of attorneys as high or very high. If that poll is representative of the population as a whole, the increase in litigation against attorneys is not very surprising.

Section III

THE LEGAL BACKGROUND

The bases of liability for errors in securities transactions are important in considering appropriate preventative measures. For example, more

13. SEC Securities Act Release No. 5404 (June 18, 1973), [1973 Transfer Binder] Fed. Sec. L. Rep. (CCH) ¶ 79,407, at n. 20.

14. SEC v. National Student Mktg. Corp., 360 F.Supp. 284 (D.D.C. 1973).

15. SEC v. National Student Mktg. Corp., [1977–78 Transfer Binder] Fed. Sec. L. Rep. (CCH) ¶ 96,027 (D.D.C. May 2, 1977). Terms of the settlement

are discussed in the text accompanying note 60 *infra*.

16. SEC v. National Student Marketing Corp., 457 F.Supp. 682 (1978).

17. Huskin v. Hindry & Meyer, The American Lawyer, Aug. 11, 1978, at 7, col. 1 (Dist. Ct. Denver, Colorado).

18. *Lawyers Liability*, The American Lawyer, Aug. 11, 1978, at 6.

19. Gallup Poll, August 22, 1976.

stringent measures are appropriate when liability may be premised upon negligence than if it requires willfulness. Unfortunately, the applicable standards are not well developed or crisply defined, and a thorough treatment of the subject is beyond the scope of this Chapter. Thus, the following discussion of the bases of liability will be summary in nature, designed only to set forth the general background for consideration of preventative measures, and not to serve as a definitive treatment of current standards.[20]

As noted earlier, this Chapter is primarily concerned with liability arising from the basic economic transaction of raising money from other people to finance a business enterprise. Thus, there will be no discussion of the potential liability arising from violation of the more specialized federal securities statutes, such as the Investment Company and Investment Advisers Acts, or the broker-dealer and proxy provisions of the Securities Exchange Act of 1934 (the "1934 Act").[21] The discussion will be divided into three principal categories: liability for violation of registration provisions, liability for violation of the disclosure provisions, and liability arising under common-law tort and contract principles. In addition, there will be a discussion of the important concept of aiding and abetting liability, which can arise under both the registration and disclosure provisions, and of the somewhat different standards that may be applicable in SEC injunctive or administrative proceedings.

A. Registration Provisions

Section 12(1) of the Securities Act of 1933 (the "1933 Act")[22] imposes liability upon any person selling a security that is neither registered under Section 5 nor exempt from registration. Subject to a one-year statute of limitations, the seller's liability for the purchaser's rescission or damages remedies is virtually absolute. In addition, there are decisions extending liability to persons other than the direct sellers, on theories (1) that they aided and abetted or (2) that their participation was sufficiently substantial that they are deemed a seller for statutory purposes.

The concept of aiding and abetting will be considered in general terms below. However, some discussion in the strict liability context of Section 12(1) is appropriate. The principal aiding and abetting case of this nature is *SEC v. Spectrum, Ltd.*[23] In that case, the attorney issued an opinion letter that facilitated an unregistered, non-exempt distribution of securities. The district court dismissed the complaint, in part on the basis of a test of actual knowledge of the improper scheme plus an intent to further that scheme. The Court of Appeals reversed, concluding that, at least

---

20. For an extensive treatment of the subject, *see* H. Bloomenthal, Securities and Federal Corporate Law (1980 Rev.) *see also* Parker, *Attorney Liability Under the Securities Law after Ernst & Ernst v. Hochfelder,* 10 Loyola L.Rev. 521 (1977). The author concludes that "while the trend moves steadily toward increased exposure of securities lawyers in their professional role, the greatest cause for concern is the sheer uncertainty." *Id.* at 583.

21. 15 U.S.C. §§ 78a *et seq.* (1980).

22. 15 U.S.C. §§ 77a *et seq.* (1980).

23. 489 F.2d 535 (2d Cir. 1973).

with respect to opinion letters, and with respect to an SEC injunctive action, a negligence standard was appropriate. *Spectrum* was an SEC enforcement action brought under Section 5 of the 1933 Act, and as is discussed under the heading *Aiding and Abetting Liability,* Section 3 below, there are cases rejecting the possibility of secondary liability under such express liability provisions as Section 12(1). However, unless and until the matter is resolved to the contrary by the appellate courts, there appears to be a significant possibility of both administrative and civil damages liability for attorney negligence contributing to registration violations.

The securities practitioner should possibly be even more concerned with the concept of the attorney as a participant in a distribution, such that he will be deemed to be a seller. Under Section 12(1), a seller has no defenses based on due care, and thus an attorney-participant could be exposed to liability even in the absence of negligence. A troubling case is *Wassel v. Eglowsky.*[24] The attorney was heavily involved in planning a transaction and, with knowledge that it would be relied upon, issued an opinion letter with respect to the free-trading status of certain securities held by controlling persons. The attorney was held liable without direct consideration of whether his opinion letter was negligently or recklessly erroneous, as is appropriate when considering the liability of a party who is a statutory seller. While the *Wassel* court focused on the extent of the attorney's participation, stating that he "did much more than simply serve as an attorney" for the issuer,[25] he had no interest in the matter other than attorneys' fees, and arguably his role was different only in modest degree from that of any attorney whose clients solicit his active assistance in planning, negotiating and effectuating transactions. Perhaps the real key to the case is that the court clearly believed the attorney had rendered his erroneous opinion recklessly or knowingly, although this state of mind was not a direct requirement for liability under the court's approach.

There are other cases bearing on the liability of attorneys under Section 12(1) as a participant, but no satisfactory limitation has emerged on the potential for liability arising from non-negligent performance of typical professional services.[26] One of the most recent cases is *SEC v. Haswell*[27] where the SEC asserted that a bond attorney was liable for violating the registration provisions based on his allegedly erroneous opinion that interest on a bond issue would be tax exempt (had the issue been tax exempt, it would also have been exempt from 1933 Act registration).[28] The court concluded, first, that there was no credible evidence that the opinion was erroneous and, second, that in the absence of negligence or recklessness, even if the opinion were erroneous and the issue had not

24. 399 F.Supp. 1330 (D. Md. 1975).

25. *Id.,* at 1368.

26. *See, e.g., SEC v. Management Dynamics, Inc.,* 515 F.2d 801 (2d Cir. 1975); *Katz v. Amos Treat & Co.,* 411 F.2d 1046 (2d Cir. 1969); *Nicewarner v. Bleavins,* 244 F.Supp. 261 (D. Col.

1965). This line of cases is discussed in Parker, *supra* note 20, at 567–77.

27. [Current Volume] Fed. Sec. L. Rep. (CCH) ¶ 97,156 (W.D. Okla. 1977).

28. *See* § 3(a)(2), clause 6, of the 1933 Act.

been exempt from registration, the attorney would not have been liable. The opinion does not directly address the issue of whether the attorney was sufficiently involved to be deemed a seller, but is helpful in its conclusion that at least negligence in rendering the erroneous opinion would be required for liability.

In considering the possibility of liability arising from legal work in unregistered offerings, it should be noted that registration is evidenced by an order of the SEC, whereas most of the exemptions are self-activating and compliance with their conditions is open to future challenge. Thus, unlike a failure to comply with all the technical requirements of a registration form or related SEC rules, the failure to comply with all technical details of an exemption can result in a registration violation and consequent exposure to the strict standards of liability under Section 12(1). Because of the attorney's possible role as a participant-seller or an aider and abettor, and also because of the attorney's potential exposure to the client for erroneous advice with respect to the exemption requirements, a rather high degree of care is appropriate when dealing with registration exemptions.

B.   Liability for Inadequate Disclosure

1.   *Section 11 Liability for Registered Offerings*

In the case of registered offerings, Section 11 of the 1933 Act prescribes standards of liability for material misstatements or omissions in the registration statement. Liability can exist to any person acquiring the security during the offering or for a substantial period of time thereafter. Persons potentially liable include the issuer, its directors, its officers who signed the registration statement, underwriters, and experts named with their consent as having prepared or certified any part of the registration statement. Under Section 11, the issuer has no defense based on the exercise of due care. Other parties do have such a defense, known as the "due diligence defense." The applicable test depends on whether or not the information has been expertised by another party. For any party with respect to non-expertised information, and for the expert with respect to information expertised by him, the defense requires a showing that after reasonable investigation the party had reasonable grounds to believe, and did believe, that the statements were true and complete; for information expertised by another party, the defense requires a showing that the party had no reasonable ground to believe, and did not believe, that the statements were untrue or misleading.

For the most part, an attorney is not an "expert" for Section 11 purposes. Exposure in this regard is typically limited to the opinion letter with respect to the validity of the securities being offered. In addition, from time to time registration statements will contain references to attorneys passing upon tax or title matters, and as to those matters such attorneys may be experts for Section 11 purposes. As for the balance of the registration statement, attorneys are not experts, although they may participate very heavily in its drafting, in the course of assisting the issuer to meet its registration and disclosure obligations.[29]

Attorneys do not sign the registration statement in their capacities as attorneys, and thus are not subject to Section 11, except as to information expertised by them. However, an attorney may play a second role in the registration process, and can be liable in that capacity. In particular, an attorney serving as a director of the issuer could be liable as a director. Moreover, several cases exploring the liability of the attorney-director indicate that because of his professional expertise and sophistication, and because of his substantial role in the registration process, he is likely to be held to a very high standard of care in order to meet his due diligence defense.[30]

2. Sections 12(2) and 17(a) of the 1933 Act

In addition to provisions prescribing liability for material misstatements or omissions in registered offerings, the 1933 Act also contains two provisions affecting material misstatements or omissions in both registered and unregistered offerings. Section 12(2) provides for liability of a seller who does not sustain the burden of proof that he did not know and, in the exercise of reasonable care, could not have known of the misstatement or omission. Because of the privity requirement, attorneys acting as such, and not involved in selling an offering, would normally not be exposed to Section 12(2) liability, other than as aiders and abettors. However, as discussed above in the context of the registration provisions, the standards for determining when an attorney's participation is sufficient for him to be deemed a "seller" are uncertain. For example, in *Katz v. Amos Treat & Co.*[31] an attorney responded in a positive manner to a private placement investor's inquiries about a company and the status of a proposed registered offering. The court held that in these circumstances a jury question was raised as to whether he was liable under Section 12(2) as a "party to a solicitation."

Section 17(a) makes it unlawful for "any person" in the offer or sale of any securities: (1) to employ any device, scheme or artifice to defraud, (2) to make any material misstatement or omission, or (3) to engage in any transaction or practice that operates as a fraud or deceit upon the purchaser. Section 17(a) does not expressly provide for liability to the purchaser, and the courts have not yet resolved the question of implied liability for its violation.[32] Until recently it was also uncertain whether a violation of Section 17(a) could be established without a showing of "scienter," which is essentially an intent to deceive or possibly a mental

---

29. Escott v. BarChris Constr. Corp., 283 F.Supp. 643, 683 (S.D.N.Y. 1968).

30. Feit v. Leasco Data Processing Equipment Corp., 332 F.Supp. 544 (E.D. N.Y. 1971); Escott v. BarChris Constr. Corp., 283 F.Supp. 643 (S.D.N.Y. 1968).

31. 411 F.2d 1046 (2d Cir. 1969).

32. *See, e.g.,* Mendelsohn v. Capital Underwriters, Inc., [Current Volume] Fed. Sec. L. Rep. (CCH) ¶ 97,169 (N.D. Cal. 1980) (no implied private right of action); Gunter v. Hutcheson, 433 F.Supp. 42 (N.D. Ga. 1977) (no implied private right of action); Surowitz v. Hilton Hotels Corp., 342 F.2d 596 (7th Cir. 1965), *rev'd on other grds.* 383 U.S. 363 (1966) (there is an implied private right of action).

state of recklessness.[33] This issue has been settled by the Supreme Court's decision in *Aaron v. SEC,*[34] which held that scienter is required to establish violations of the first clause set out above, but not of the second and third clauses. Violations of Section 17(a) can serve as the basis of SEC injunctive or disciplinary proceedings.

3. *Rule 10b-5 under the 1934 Act*

Rule 10b-5 under the 1934 Act makes it illegal to employ any device, scheme or artifice to defraud, to make any material misstatement or omission, or to engage in any act, practice, or course of business which operates as a fraud or deceit upon any person in connection with the purchase or sale of a security. It is firmly established that Rule 10b-5 will support a private action for damages, but that proof of scienter is required for either private damages or an SEC injunction.[35] As applied by a number of courts, it appears that the scienter requirement can be met by proof of recklessness.[36]

The scienter requirement aside, Rule 10b-5 is more flexible than many of the other liability provisions, especially with respect to the privity requirement and the class of persons who may be liable, and thus it is frequently involved in allegations of attorney liability. In addition, many of the aiding and abetting cases, and some of the most troubling SEC enforcement actions involving attorneys, have arisen under Rule 10b-5.

C. Aiding and Abetting Liability

As is obvious from a review of the foregoing liability provisions, they frequently are not specifically applicable to persons acting in the traditional role of the attorney in securities transactions. However, in reality that role tends to be of substantial and at times pervasive importance. For these reasons, aiding and abetting concepts are an important source of exposure of attorneys to liability under the federal securities laws.

Some courts have held that aiding and abetting liability is not available under certain of the securities law liability provisions, on the ground that such secondary liability would circumvent the specific liability limitations appearing in Sections 11 and 12 of the 1933 Act.[37] The authors believe these cases are correctly decided. However, aiding and abetting concepts have been accepted by courts in several SEC and private damages actions under other provisions of the securities laws,[38] and such concepts have also

33. *See, e.g.,* SEC v. American Realty Trust, 586 F.2d 1001 (2d Cir. 1978) (scienter not required in SEC injunctive action); Sanders v. John Nuveen & Co., Inc., 554 F.2d 790 (7th Cir. 1977) (scienter required in private action).

34. 100 S.Ct. 1945, —— U.S. —— (1980).

35. Aaron v. SEC. *Id.*; Ernst & Ernst v. Hochfelder, 425 U.S. 185 (1976).

36. *See, e.g.,* Coleco Industries v. Berman, 567 F.2d 569, 574 (3d Cir. 1977), and the discussion and citations at Ar-

nold S. Jacobs, *Rule 10b-5 Developments—Who Can Sue and Who is Liable?,* PLI Tenth Annual Institute on Securities Regulation 457, 466–69 (1978).

37. *See* In Re: Equity Funding Corp. of America SEC Litigation, 416 F.Supp. 161, 181 (C.D. Cal. 1976). *See also,* Kobil v. Forsberg, 389 F.Supp. 715, 718 (W.D. Pa. 1975).

38. *See, e.g.,* SEC v. Universal Major Industries Corp., 546 F.2d 1044 (2d Cir. 1976) (attorney as aider and abettor of

been accepted in the criminal context. Absent Supreme Court action, aiding and abetting should therefore be considered a significant source of exposure to liability under Sections 11 and 12. This is especially true in certain factual situations where an attorney may be perceived as the only "deep pocket."

In general, liability as an aider and abettor would arise if an attorney willfully takes actions, otherwise legal, knowing that such actions substantially assist illegal actions on the part of another person. In addition, and this is where the matter becomes particularly difficult, liability can arise where the attorney should have known of the illegal venture. It is unclear, at least in SEC actions, whether mere negligent failure to discern the illegality is sufficient.[39]

Because of aiding and abetting concepts, an attorney involved in a securities transaction cannot safely close his eyes to other parts of the transaction. While it is generally agreed that participation in one aspect of a securities transaction does not impose an obligation to closely scrutinize the entire transaction, it is also clear that an attorney who focuses solely on one aspect, without some sensitivity to obvious misuse of his work product, is subject to aiding and abetting exposure on the ground that he should have known of the violation that his participation helped make possible.[40] Of course, an attorney approaching these matters should be aware that a defense based upon lack of knowledge or notice of the primary violation would have to withstand the harsh, and possibly unfair, light of hindsight.

D.   Common-Law Malpractice Liability

As is true of any attorney-client relationship, an attorney involved in securities transactions has duties which, if breached, can render him liable to the client. In general, the attorney is responsible under contract principles to exercise reasonable skill, care and diligence in rendering the services which he agrees to perform. He also may be subject to common-

Section 5 violations); Adams v. Standard Knitting Mills, Inc., [1976 Transfer Binder] Fed. Sec. L. Rep. (CCH) ¶ 95,-683 (E.D. Tenn. 1976); Lorber v. Beebe, 407 F.Supp. 279, 287–88 and note 6 (S.D.N.Y. 1975).

39. *See* SEC v. Spectrum, 489 F.2d 535, 541 (2d Cir. 1973). For a case rejecting *Spectrum's* negligence standard, requiring "general awareness" that the attorney's role was part of an overall improper activity, and also requiring knowing and substantial assistance in the face of such general awareness, *see* SEC v. Coffey, 493 F.2d 1304, 1316 (6th Cir. 1974). *Coffey* does suggest that aiding and abetting liability could arise if one "had reason to suspect" that a violation would occur, but does not explore the nature of circumstances that would be deemed to provide reason for

suspicion. *See* Chappell & Cheek, n. 3, *supra*, 281–86; Johnson & Wheeler, *Securities Law Duties of Bond Counsel,* 1976 Duke L. J. 1205 (exploring the question in the context of the duties of bond counsel called upon to render a necessary opinion but not to otherwise participate in the preparation of offering documents).

40. *See, e.g.,* Loeker Landau, *Legal Opinions Rendered in Securities Transactions,* PLI Eighth Annual Institute on Securities Regulation 3 (1977); *Report by Special Committee, infra* note 107, at 1888 (Guideline 4); ABA Comm. on Professional Ethics, Opinion No. 335 (1974). Chappell & Cheek, *supra* note 3 (including comments by Stanley Sporkin, Director, SEC Division of Enforcement, at 284–86).

law tort actions if he fails to render services with the degree of care called for by the "reasonable man" standard. In the case of attorneys holding themselves out to be specialists in a particular area, the standard of comparison is the skill, care and diligence of specialists in that area.

There is little reported authority concerning liability of attorneys to their securities law clients for errors resulting in the client's liability under the securities laws. However, such exposure is present. For example, in *BarChris Construction Corp.,* the clients cross-claimed against the attorneys; these claims were settled.[41] It appears that attorneys have little, if any, exposure to claims by non-clients for common-law malpractice in connection with securities transactions.[42]

E. SEC Injunctive and Disciplinary Proceedings

The securities law practitioner must also be very conscious of the possibility of SEC enforcement actions, either in the form of suits for injunctive relief or disciplinary proceedings under SEC Rule 2(e).

The seriousness of any injunctive proceeding, even one that might result in relatively innocuous proscriptions, has been heightened by the Supreme Court's decision in *Parklane Hosiery.*[43] Under that case, factual findings by the court in SEC injunctive proceedings have a collateral estoppel effect in subsequent civil damages actions, and thus can be used against the attorney by private parties. It should also be noted that regardless of whether Section 17(a) of the 1933 Act will support a private damages action, the SEC clearly is an appropriate party for seeking relief under that Section,[44] and need not prove scienter to establish violations of paragraphs 17(a)(2) and (3).[45]

Rule 2(e)[46] provides that the Commission can deny the privilege of appearing before it if a person is shown (i) not to possess the requisite qualifications to represent others, or (ii) to be lacking in character or integrity or to have engaged in unethical or improper professional conduct, or (iii) to have willfully violated, or willfully aided and abetted the violation of the federal securities laws. Despite the absence of clear statutory authority,[47] and despite a chorus of professional and academic criticism,[48] the SEC has been utilizing Rule 2(e) proceedings with increas-

41. *See* 3A H. Bloomenthal, Securities and Federal Corporate Law § 8.17 (1980 Rev.).

42. *See* Goodman v. Kennedy, 18 Cal.3d 335, 134 Cal.Rptr. 375, 556 P.2d 737 (1976); *see also* Amey v. Henderson, Franklin, Starnes & Holt, P.A., 367 So.2d 633 (Fla.App. 1979).

43. Parklane Hosiery Co., Inc. v. Shore, 439 U.S. 322, [1979 Transfer Binder] Fed. Sec. L. Rep. (CCH) ¶ 96,713 (1979).

44. *See, e.g.,* Aaron v. SEC, 100 S.Ct. 1945, —— U.S. —— (1980); SEC v. Texas Gulf Sulphur, 401 F.2d 833, 867 (2d Cir. 1968) (Friendly, J., concurring).

45. Aaron v. SEC. *Id.*

46. 17 C.F.R. § 201.2(e) (1979).

47. *See* the dissent of Com'r Roberta S. Karmel in *In re* Keating, Muething & Klekamp, SEC Securities Exchange Act Release No. 15982 (July 2, 1979), 511 SEC. REG. L. REP. (BNA) E-1, E-6 (July 11, 1979).

48. *See, e.g.,* Downy & Miller, *The Distortion and Misuse of Rule 2(e),* 54 N.D. Law. 774 (1979); Michael R. Klein, *The SEC and the Legal Profession: Material Adverse Developments,* PLI Eleventh Annual Institute on Securities Regulation 597, 630–44 (1979).

ing frequency to deal with professionals, including attorneys, it believes have not met satisfactory standards of practice.[49] While these proceedings cannot result in factual findings having collateral estoppel effect in private damages actions, the suspension of the right to practice before the Commission can be a very serious sanction. As interpreted by the SEC, this sanction not only precludes attorneys from participating in filings or appearances before the Commission, but may also generally preclude the rendering of advice and assistance in federal securities law matters.[50] Professional concern with Rule 2(e) proceedings has been heightened by the applicable standard of proof (preponderance of the evidence), restrictive discovery rules, absence of a scienter requirement, and restrictions on the matters that may properly be the subject of rebuttal evidence.[51]

F. Overview of Liability Standards

There is no simple way in which to summarize the legal standards under which an attorney may be held liable as a result of errors in securities law transactions. A standard of actual knowledge, intent to defraud, or at least recklessness, is applicable to several important sources of potential liability, including Rule 10b-5 and general concepts of aiding and abetting. Moreover, despite widespread concern, there is a dearth of actual cases in which attorneys have been held liable for damages to non-clients on a showing of negligence, and even SEC proceedings in which a negligence standard is endorsed typically involve facts that could fairly be characterized as going beyond negligence.[52]

Nonetheless, with multiple sources of liability, and the uncertainty with respect to applicable standards of care as to many of them, negligent errors create significant exposure to both administrative proceedings and liability (or at least litigation as to liability) to the investing public and/or the client. In addition, errors with respect to the exempt status of unregistered offerings carry some potential for exposure regardless of the level of care, if the attorney is sufficiently involved to be deemed a statutory seller—itself a matter of some uncertainty.[53]

Exposure in securities transactions is increased by the number of parties, and thus potential litigants, involved in those transactions, and by

---

49. *See* the summary of Rule 2(e) proceedings set forth in Klein, *supra* note 48, at 608–30.

50. Rule 2(g) states that "practicing before the Commission shall include, but not be limited to" transacting business with the Commission or preparing documents filed with consent with another document. *But see*, the settlement terms in *In re* Stanley T. Traska, SEC Securities Act Release No. 5617 (Sept. 18, 1975), and *In re* Robert A. Petrallia, et al., SEC Securities Release No. 5963 (Aug. 25, 1978).

51. *See, e.g.,* Downy and Miller, *supra* note 48.

52. For example, in SEC v. Coffey, 493 F.2d 1304 (6th Cir. 1974), the court rejected the negligence standard in aiding and abetting situations, but nonetheless stated its view, at note 30, that the *Spectrum* decision, *supra* note 39, was properly decided on its facts, particularly because the attorney was "aware that the misleading opinion could be used to sell unregistered securities and failed to take timely steps to prevent such use." 493 F.2d, at 1316, note 30.

53. *See Registration Provisions,* Section III. A., *supra.*

the settlement leverage created by diverse and uncertain standards of liability. We believe that these factors call for careful consideration of policies and procedures designed to prevent errors in the first place. These policies and procedures should also be beneficial in establishing a state-of-mind defense (whether the standard be actual knowledge, intent, negligence or otherwise) in the event errors do occur. We also believe that such a program can reduce the likelihood of an SEC action against a firm in the event of an error, or at least may serve as the basis of a satisfactory negotiated settlement (as reflected in the SEC enforcement actions discussed in Section IV below).

Further, a program designed to prevent errors in securities transactions will bear on the likelihood of future violations, and thus on whether injunctive relief is appropriate. Of course, cessation of past conduct is not a complete defense to an action for equitable relief, even if the cessation occurred prior to the institution of the action.[54] However, from a preventative viewpoint, the focus is on evidence that future violations will not occur even if a court does not issue an injunction or grant other relief.[55] Because good faith implementation of various preventative policies and procedures does demonstrate that a law firm is policing itself, even if an inadvertent error has occurred, it will constitute evidence that future violations will not occur.

It must be emphasized, however, that institution of particular procedures to be followed in all similar transactions, and even of particular procedures for particular transactions, must be done with the same intelligence and sensitivity to the particular factual circumstances that should characterize all legal work in connection with securities transactions. The institution of a procedure that is impractically burdensome may result in its not being followed, which could enhance exposure for failure to exert the level of care that the attorneys themselves have, by instituting the procedure, deemed appropriate in the circumstances. Further, procedures must supplement and serve as a check on an attorney's careful and thoughtful discharge of responsibilities, and not become the standard, in an attorney's own mind, for whether those responsibilities have in fact been discharged. That is, proceduralization must not preempt the exercise of judgment, care and discretion, whether or not a matter is readily the subject of a procedure. For these reasons, a significant portion of the following treatment will be concerned not with step-by-step procedures to be instituted, but with broader policy questions of client selection, and the qualifications of attorneys and their general mental approach to a securities transaction. To the extent that we deal with procedural suggestions, it is important that their selection for particular transactions or classes of transactions be the result of a properly trained, conscientious attorney's judgment that such procedures are appropriate in the particular circumstances.

54. *E.g.*, Hecht Co. v. Bowles, 321 U.S. 321, 327 (1943).

55. *See, e.g.*, SEC v. National Student Mktg. Corp., [1977–78 Transfer Binder] Fed. Sec. L. Rep. (CCH) ¶ 96,027 (D.D.C. 1977), in which the court denied the SEC's request for a preliminary injunction.

The implementation of policies and procedures does entail the expenditure of time and money by attorneys, a great deal of which is certain to be passed on to clients in the form of either higher hourly rates or billings for a greater number of hours. Of course, clients are the direct beneficiaries of any procedures that reduce errors in their securities transactions, because of the consequent reduction in litigation and associated expense and uncertainty; whether the benefit they receive equals the additional cost is a speculative matter which we do not seek to resolve. In any event, the cost of policies and procedures reasonably necessary to ensure compliance with the securities laws, and to protect the attorneys who provide advice about those laws, is plainly a legitimate cost of our system of regulating securities transactions.

Section IV

OVERVIEW OF THE DEFENSIVE PRACTICE OF LAW AS OUTLINED BY SETTLEMENTS IN SEC ACTIONS

To gain a perspective on law firm policies and procedures that may prevent errors in securities transactions, it is useful to review a few of the recent SEC administrative and injunctive actions against both attorneys and accountants. The actions discussed below entail settlements with the SEC based upon the implementation of a series of new or improved firm policies and procedures. In reviewing these procedures, it should be understood that the SEC does not claim general authority to specify the manner in which law firms render their services. However, various of its proceedings against attorneys, as well as positions stated by members of its staff, make clear that it expects firms to follow procedures of their own choosing sufficient to properly discharge their responsibilities.[56] Presumably, procedures included in settlements are believed by the SEC to be reasonably tailored to this goal.

Two recent administrative actions against accountants are also included in the following discussion. There appears to be a growing tendency to view the responsibilities of attorneys and accountants in a similar light.[57] Thus, while there are substantial differences in the tasks and statutory

56. Comments to this effect were made at the "SEC Speaks in 1980" PLI program held on March 7–8, 1980, by Paul Gonson, Solicitor to the Commission, in connection with a panel discussion of *In re* Keating, Muething & Klekamp, SEC Securities Exchange Act Release No. 15982 (July 2, 1979). Comments by Staff members represent their own views and not necessarily those of the SEC.

57. *See* Hager, *SEC Chief to Lawyers: You May Be Next,* Legal Times of Washington, Aug. 14, 1978 at 1, col. 2. In a speech to the ABA convention in New York in August 1978, SEC Chairman Harold Williams stated:

> I would commend to your careful study the drama which is continuing to unfold concerning whether regulation of the independent accounting profession should be made a subject of federal legislation . . . ..
> It provides a clear and very relevant illustration of how the public and the legislative branch may seek to remedy perceived ills in the corporate sector with nostrums directed

responsibilities of attorneys and accountants in securities transactions, attorneys can benefit from an awareness of settlements with accountants, especially in the broad area of quality control.

The first significant administrative action by the SEC against a law firm involving a settlement based upon the implementation of corrective and remedial policies and procedures was *In re Jo M. Ferguson.*[58] This was a Rule 2(e)[59] proceeding based upon a failure by bond counsel to include certain material facts in the offering circular. The remedial policies and procedures adopted by the attorney and his firm were extensive. The settlement included the following terms:

(1) Every two weeks, members of the firm must meet and discuss all of their active cases. Affirmative approval of *each* partner is required before the issuance of any legal opinion in a securities transaction.

(2) The firm must undertake an appropriate investigation in connection with acting as bond counsel including, among other things, obtaining independently audited financial statements and inquiring into the background of the various parties connected with the offering. Written evidence of those investigations and the results thereof must be reviewed by the partners of the firm.

(3) An appropriate "engagement letter" must be sent to all interested parties, emphasizing that the firm's duty is to the issuer and the bondholders. It must define the scope of the firm's work as bond counsel and require submission to it of certain pertinent information.

(4) The firm must require that it receive independently audited financial statements for lessees and guarantors, representations from appropriately interested persons concerning the accuracy and completeness of the statements about them in any offering circular, and a statement from counsel for any lessee or guarantor that counsel has reviewed the offering circular and is aware of no inaccuracies therein.

(5) Each partner and associate of the firm must attend a municipal bond workshop or seminar on at least one occasion each year.

One of the more striking aspects of this settlement is the requirement that each partner in the firm approve every opinion rendered in securities transactions. It is important, however, to note that the firm in the *Ferguson* case was small. This procedure clearly would not be appropriate for all firms because of the varying number of partners and associates, the scope of their securities practice, the experience and abilities of clients and attorneys, the degree of supervision customarily provided to less experienced attorneys, and numerous other factors.

---

to those who render professional service to the business community. I suggest that, for these purposes, the similarities between the legal and accounting professions far outweigh their differences.

58. SEC Securities Act Release No. 5523 (Aug. 21, 1974), 5 SEC Docket 37.

59. *See* the discussion at *SEC Injunctive and Disciplinary Proceedings,* Section III, Section E, *supra.*

A more recent case that resulted in a settlement with attorneys based on compliance with preventative policies and procedures was *SEC v. National Student Marketing Corp.*[60] This case was the first SEC enforcement action against a large, nationally prominent law firm, and the nature of the preventative measures reflects not only the radically different practice from that of the firm in *Jo M. Ferguson,* but also the particular circumstances of the transaction leading to the SEC's complaint. The settlement was based on a letter from the firm to the SEC confirming the procedures then in force in securities transactions. It set forth nine major categories of policies and procedures, which are summarized below:

(1) A committee of partners is responsible for approving any new representation when the firm acts as principal outside counsel in a securities transaction involving registration under the federal securities laws. If the committee ascertains that prior outside counsel resigned, an inquiry will be made as to the basis of the resignation. The firm will request the prospective client to release the prior counsel from any obligation of confidentiality in order to discuss the proposed representation. A written record is to be maintained of this type of investigation.[61]

(2) Prior to undertaking the representation as principal outside counsel of a prospective client having securities registered under the federal securities laws, the responsible partner will determine whether a Report on Form 8-K[62] has been filed within the previous two years reflecting a change in independent public accountants. A committee of partners will review any such change and determine whether an inquiry of the prior independent public accountant is required. If it is determined that one is required, the prospective client will be asked to direct the prior accountant to respond to inquiries by the firm, and the entire analysis will be documented and maintained by the firm.

(3) When the firm represents the issuer of securities, it will not deliver an opinion in connection with the issue if it has knowledge (i) that any material representation or warranty made by or on behalf of the client is not true and correct in light of the circumstances under which it was made, or (ii) that there has been any material adverse change that would render any such representation or warranty false or misleading after the date the transaction is closed.

---

60. [1977–78 Transfer Binder] Fed. Sec. L. Rep. (CCH) ¶ 96,027 (D.D.C. May 2, 1977).

61. Of some interest is the lack of any requirement that the committee investigate situations in which the client has dismissed prior outside counsel. However, the authors believe that the SEC would consider this an implied term of the settlement.

62. Companies whose securities are listed on an exchange and those registered under § 12(g) of the 1934 Securities Exchange Act must file Reports on Form 8-K within 15 days of certain occurrences, including changes in independent public accountants. 17 C.F.R. §§ 240.13a-11 and 249.308.

(4) If the firm becomes aware during the course of a transaction involving the issuance of securities to the public of any false or misleading representation or warranty by or on behalf of the client, the firm will advise the client of its disclosure obligations under the federal securities laws. If a client does not take appropriate action, the partner in charge of the transaction will consider with at least two other partners whether the firm must withdraw or take other action.

(5) When the firm represents an issuer participating in a transaction in which securities are issued to the public, and if the terms of the transaction call for the delivery of documents dealing with the issuer's financial condition, if any party to the transaction elects to waive delivery of such documentation or to accept it in a form that does not comply with the terms of the transaction, the firm will not render any opinion in connection with the transaction until the partner responsible for the transaction has consulted with and obtained the concurrence of at least two other partners.

(6) When the firm represents an issuer or underwriter of securities in a transaction involving the issuance of securities to the public, registration statements prepared by the firm will be reviewed by a second partner who is not directly involved in the transaction. In addition, any opinion delivered by the firm will reasonably identify the matter upon which the opinion is being rendered and describe the nature of the review upon which the opinion is based.

(7) In connection with any transaction involving the issuance of securities to the public, if the firm is requested to deliver an opinion with respect to the effective date of such transaction and the responsible partner becomes aware that the date or dates of any events comprising or affecting in any significant way such transaction are other than as reflected in the documents relating to such transaction, such partner will (i) ascertain the reason and purpose for any such variance in dates, (ii) review the matter with another partner of the firm, and (iii) state in any opinion delivered the extent to which such variance in dates may affect the legal conclusions set forth in such opinion.

(8) In communicating with independent public accountants, the firm will comply with the guidelines established by the *ABA Statement of Policy Regarding Lawyers' Responses to Auditors' Requests for Information* [63] and the accompanying commentary.

(9) The firm will continue to encourage partners and associates to participate in legal education programs dealing with corporate and securities law developments. In addition, the firm will make available to the attorneys dealing with corporate and securities law the current materials on those matters.

The additional scope and detail of the *National Student Marketing* settlement, compared to the *Ferguson* settlement, reflect many of the

63. 31 Bus. Law. 1709–45 (1976).

factors that distinguish law firms from each other, but may also reflect a developing intention of the SEC to hold law firms representing issuers of securities to the same type of formal quality control procedures that are more traditional in the accounting profession.[64] A review of two recent settlements in Rule 2(e) cases with accountants will demonstrate that the SEC's expectations in this regard can go well beyond the audit-related procedures that are required by generally accepted auditing standards.

In re Seidman & Seidman [65] concerned a merger of Seidman & Seidman with the Los Angeles accounting firm of Wolfson, Weiner, Ratoff & Lapin, as well as the audits of certain clients of the latter firm, including Equity Funding Corporation of America. The opinion and order in this action are extremely detailed and lengthy; however the offer of settlement by Seidman & Seidman that was accepted by the Commission can be reviewed, and utilized, without a detailed understanding of the entire opinion. Seidman & Seidman agreed to conduct an in-depth examination and evaluation of its audit policies, procedures, and practices, and to report its determinations to the Commission. The areas to be analyzed included the following:

(1) hiring practices for all professionals;

(2) training and education for all professionals;

(3) promotion and compensation of all professionals;

(4) acceptance and retention of clients;

(5) setting and recovery of audit engagement fees;

(6) allocation of professional responsibilities within the firm;

(7) professional staffing of files;

(8) maintenance of professional independence;

(9) conduct of audit practice engagements, including staffing, allocation of responsibilities, work paper preparation and review, interoffice communications, identification and resolution of problems, independent review procedures, and outside expertise;

(10) formulation of firm practices, procedures, and policies, and communication of these to professionals in the firm;

(11) creation and implementation of quality controls;

(12) firmwide correction or improvement measures;

(13) criteria and procedures to analyze potential merger or combination of practice candidates; and

---

64. Several other recent SEC actions involving settlements with attorneys are useful to review. *See In re* Keating, Muething & Klekamp, SEC Securities Exchange Act Release No. 15982 (July 2, 1979); SEC v. Petrofunds, Inc., SEC Litigation Release No. 8001 (S.D.N.Y. June 28, 1977), 12 SEC Docket 1093 (for a summary of this litigation, *see* [1977–78 Transfer Binder] Fed. Sec. L. Rep. (CCH) ¶ 96,098); *In re* Plotkin, Yolles, Siegel & Turner, SEC Securities Act Release No. 5841 (July 5, 1977),

[1977–78 Transfer Binder] Fed. Sec. L. Rep. (CCH) ¶ 81,236; SEC v. Geo Dynamics Oil & Gas, Inc., [1975–76 Transfer Binder] Fed. Sec. L. Rep. (CCH) ¶ 95,565 (D.D.C. June 1, 1976); *In re* McLaughlin, Stern, Ballen & Miller, SEC Securities Exchange Act Release No. 11,553 (1975).

65. SEC Securities Exchange Act Release No. 12,752 (Sept. 1, 1976), 5 Fed. Sec. L. Rep. (CCH) ¶ 72,218.

(14) allocation and exercise of responsibilities by various committees of the firm.

Another recent Rule 2(e) proceeding involving accountants that reflects the same type of detailed settlement is *In re Laventhol & Horwath*.[66] In essence, this settlement provided for the same analysis of the audit practice as was set forth in the *Seidman & Seidman* settlement. The only significant difference is that no provision was made for a combination or merger with other firms, reflecting the differing factual bases of the two proceedings.

The settlement provisions set forth in *Ferguson, National Student Marketing, Seidman & Seidman,* and *Laventhol & Horwath* provide an overview of areas in which the SEC apparently believes policies and procedures can help prevent errors in securities transactions. In general, they may be divided into the following broad categories, each of which we will discuss at some length in the balance of this Chapter:

1. Policies and procedures designed to evaluate the client, its background, the nature of the transaction, and the relationship with the law firm (for example, the client review committee in *National Student Marketing,* and the engagement letter and background inquiry requirements in *Ferguson*).

2. Policies and procedures designed to ensure appropriate legal and factual investigation with respect to opinion letters (for example, the requirement in *Ferguson* that all partners approve opinions, and in *National Student Marketing* that certain matters be addressed in securities transaction opinions).

3. Policies and procedures designed to ensure compliance with applicable disclosure and registration/exemption requirements (for example, second partner review in *National Student Marketing,* and the factual inquiry requirements in *Ferguson*).

4. Policies and procedures designed to enhance attorney competence (for example, the continuing legal education requirements in both *Ferguson* and *National Student Marketing*).

In addition, the discussion that follows will address policies and procedures designed to identify, resolve or control conflicts of interests, and to identify the presence of a security in a business transaction.

Section V

THE CLIENT: IDENTIFICATION AND EVALUATION

A. Identification

In securities transactions, firms should consider a procedure for identifying and evaluating clients, especially when dealing with new clients.

66. SEC Accounting Release No. 227 (Sept. 21, 1977), 5 Fed. Sec. L. Rep. (CCH) ¶ 72,249.

Although it sounds simplistic, evaluation of a client cannot be done until the identification is completed. The process of identification includes the recognition of those parties with whom the firm has an express agreement and generally from whom fees will be received. It also includes the recognition of other persons who may assert and successfully maintain that they stand in the position of clients.

The identification of individuals and entities that the firm has expressly agreed to represent is generally not difficult. There exist, however, situations where a firm knows the legal work directly concerns a particular individual or entity, but mistakenly decides that there is no attorney-client relationship solely because it does not receive payment for fees and expenses from that particular individual or entity. While many of these situations fall into the area of third-party beneficiaries,[67] in other situations an actual attorney-client relationship may be held to exist based on principles of implied contract.

Perhaps the best example of this situation occurred in a non-securities case, *Fort Myers Seafood Packers, Inc. v. Steptoe & Johnson.*[68] The attorneys in that case regularly represented a seafood packer and did so in a transaction involving an agreement with a commercial fishing company. The latter did not make any agreement to pay fees and expenses, but was participating in contract negotiations to provide fish to the seafood packer. The law firm prepared documents connected with registration of the commercial fishing company's vessels. Based on a lack of proper registration, certain fishing vessels were seized by a foreign country, causing direct damages to the commercial fishing company as well as indirect damages because of its inability to fulfill the terms of the contract. The court held that the commercial fishing company was a client and had standing, essentially based on an implied contract, to institute an action for negligence against the defendant law firm.

Similar situations may arise in securities transactions. For example, real estate syndications frequently involve general partners, limited partners, and real estate brokers (and perhaps promoters who are not within the previous categories). A law firm may be counsel to the general partnership or to the general partner, and also prepare legal documents that cover the involvement of additional parties such as limited partners, real estate brokers or promoters. This provides ample opportunity for an attorney-client relationship to be established even though the firm and the "client" never expressly entered into such a relationship and even though the "client" does not pay any fees or expenses.[69]

---

67. *See, e.g.* Goodman v. Kennedy, 18 Cal.3d 355, 134 Cal.Rptr. 375, 556 P.2d 737 (1976); *cf.* White v. Guarente, 43 N.Y.2d 356, 401 N.Y.S.2d 474, 372 N.E.2d 315 (1977) (concerning reliance by limited partners upon an audit by an accountant employed by the general partners).

68. 381 F.2d 261 (D.C. Cir. 1967), *cert. denied* 390 U.S. 946 (1968); *see* Annot., 18 A.L.R.3d 978 (1968).

69. *See, e.g.*, Roberts v. Ball, Hunt, Hart, Brown & Baerwitz, 57 Cal.App.3d 104, 128 Cal.Rptr. 901 (1976).

The principal concern in these situations is to clearly delineate the extent of the firm's responsibility, if any, to the various parties, so that it can evaluate the risk of the representation, and can determine appropriate staffing and procedures for delivering proper legal services. The most direct procedure is to send a letter to the various interested parties specifically defining the firm's role, including but not limited to a delineation of those individuals or entities it represents *and* those it does not represent (a non-engagement letter). Letters of this type are especially appropriate when a party having a material interest in the transaction is not represented by counsel. In these circumstances, the firm may wish to urge the unrepresented party to seek independent counsel except to the extent that the firm is willing to undertake selected multiple representation.

In most securities transactions, potential claimants will file suit under specific statutes that provide standing. Only if these statutes are not available will litigants resort to third-party beneficiary theories. Two recent California cases are instructive concerning the circumstances in which courts may permit third parties to have standing. Because California has consistently been the most flexible jurisdiction in conferring standing on third-party beneficiaries in actions against attorneys, the comparison of the following cases should provide a useful perspective on the maximum potential exposure to those claims.

In *Roberts v. Ball, Hunt, Hart, Brown & Baerwitz*,[70] a law firm was held liable to a third party for negligent misrepresentation based on a statement in an opinion letter that its client was a general partnership. The evidence reflected that certain members of the alleged partnership disputed its status and the law firm did not disclose this in the opinion. The law firm knew that the client would not only attempt to obtain a loan using the opinion letter, but would request the loan from the plaintiff. The client defaulted on the loan, and the resulting damages included the expenses incurred in instituting actions against the alleged partners, since those actions would not have been instituted but for the negligent representation of the defendant.

A few months later, in *Goodman v. Kennedy*,[71] the California Supreme Court held that purchasers of securities lacked standing to sue the attorney for the sellers based upon negligent advice that he gave to his clients. The advice consisted of representations that the securities being sold to the plaintiffs-purchasers could be resold by them without interfering with an exemption from registration under Regulation A of the Securities Act of 1933.[72]

The court held that an attorney's duty in this type of transaction does not extend to persons with whom the client dealt, at least when the client acted at arm's-length and the legal advice rendered to the client was not foreseeably relied upon by the plaintiff. Of particular importance in

---

70. *Id.*

71. 18 Cal.3d 355, 134 Cal.Rptr. 375, 556 P.2d 737 (1976).

72. 17 C.F.R. §§ 230.251–.264 (1979).

Goodman was the evidence of prior discussions between the defendant law firm and attorneys representing the plaintiffs. The plaintiffs' independent representation was important in determining the likelihood of reliance and in evaluating whether third-party beneficiary principles should be applied to provide standing.[73]

B. Evaluation

There are numerous reasons for evaluating a prospective securities client, some of which are independent of securities laws liability exposure. For example, a firm would normally want to determine whether there are actual or potential conflicts of interests with other clients or representations. Similarly, a client with a history of changing attorneys may be expected to be hard to satisfy, at least without a greater commitment of resources than can normally be justified. Aside from these considerations, evaluating a client can also be an important aspect of determining the firm's securities law exposure, and in determining the procedures that are appropriate to properly handle the representation.

In approaching the evaluation of the prospective client, several points should be considered. First, although SEC enforcement actions will sometimes occur without regard to whether a transaction resulted in a financial loss, in general the transaction that is successful presents markedly lower exposure to liability. Obviously, private investors in a successful venture are either not inclined to sue or have little basis for alleging damages, and a successful investment is less likely to be brought to the attention of the SEC enforcement staff.

Second, a prospective client's unsatisfactory background, whether related to prior illegal transactions or inadequate experience, does not itself preclude that client from proceeding with a securities transaction, or a law firm from representing that client. However, such a background may have a substantial bearing on whether, as a policy matter, a particular law firm is willing to be involved in a transaction with that prospective client, under any circumstances.

Third, an unsatisfactory background bears on both the venture's prospect for success, and also the nature of disclosures and the extent of inquiry that may be required. Thus, the client's background should be considered by a firm in setting, at the outset, the ground rules for the representation. For example, before accepting representation of a client with an insufficient or questionable background, a firm would normally want to discuss with the prospective client the types of disclosures that would be required. A firm would also want to consider the extent of necessary inquiry, and the possibility that the representation may be terminated, in setting the basis and terms of its compensation.

73. California law in this area has generated a line of cases that involved disputes over wills and trusts, beginning with Biakanja v. Irving, 49 Cal.2d 647, 320 P.2d 16 (1958) and Lucas v. Hamm, 56 Cal.2d 583, 364 P.2d 685, 15 Cal. Rptr. 821 (1961), *cert. denied* 368 U.S. 987 (1962), but more recently has involved commercial or securities cases such as *Roberts, supra* note 69 and *Goodman, supra* note 67.

As suggested by the preceding brief discussion of the relevance of client evaluation, there are four principal areas that deserve consideration, and in some circumstances serious analysis. First, a firm should inquire into the client's relationships with prior attorneys and accountants, and particularly the circumstances involved in terminating those relationships. Although the prospective client's explanation of the termination may be convincing, the fact that a difficulty arose may suggest that special efforts should be taken to prevent a recurrence of the problem. For example, if a disclosure dispute arose with the former attorney, special attention and discussion should be devoted at the outset to the particular issue that arose. In addition, the discussion should include the firm's general expectations with respect to disclosure, and the nature of disclosure that should be expected in identifiable areas of sensitivity, such as related party transactions, prior business failures, or lack of basis for projected results. Similarly, in such circumstances, the firm should consider placing special emphasis on provisions in an engagement letter concerning fees and withdrawal. Payment in advance, or as the work progresses, with clear provisions for withdrawal if disputes arise over disclosure items, will not only reduce the economic impact on the firm should a dispute arise, but also relieve the firm of a potential source of diminished objectivity in making difficult judgments about such matters.

Prior disagreements with accountants, especially those that resulted in a change in accountants, are also important to consider. Disputes with accountants over preparation of financial statements or other documents are probably as reliable an indicator of potential disclosure problems as disputes with prior attorneys. If the prospective client is publicly-held, it should have filed a Report on Form 8-K regarding the change in independent public accountants. This Report would include information about certain accounting disagreements, requires that the accountants state their agreement or disagreement with the contents of the Report, and is a source of information that would normally be somewhat more carefully and thoughtfully phrased than the client's subsequent oral explanation.

Second, it is important to assess the business history of the client and the experience of the individuals who will be managing the venture, including prior business failures and involvement in litigation with investors or the SEC. This bears not only on the likelihood of success, but also on the probable reliability of business-related information and projections provided by the client. Further, it also bears on whether prior business failures or lack of experience are material and thus must be disclosed; because clients can be particularly sensitive about disclosures of this nature, inquiry and discussion at the initial stages are appropriate.

In considering the background and abilities of the management team, the firm may wish to reach some conclusion about the ability of those individuals to identify and recruit other experienced and qualified managers. This inquiry will probably not have significant impact on the disclosure process, since the information is at best impressionistic and speculative. However, the ability to sustain the quality of management as an enterprise grows is a critical element in determining its future success, and thus should be of interest to an attorney who seeks representations having long-term potential. This point can be especially important for a relatively new venture that is meeting initial success. While the initial promoter's enthusiasm and hard work may have generated strong initial sales growth, often a different and more sophisticated management team is required to raise the enterprise to higher volume plateaus.

Third, consideration should be given to the success of similar business ventures. This information may make a difference on certain disclosure items, since adverse industry trends would normally be material. It will also give the firm information from which to determine the likelihood of financial success of the venture. Of course, a pattern of success of similar ventures should not be allowed to obscure any recent lack of success that a particular industry may have experienced. Also, differences and similarities between the business in question and other similar ventures should be examined in considering whether the industry pattern is useful as a predictor of the success of the venture at hand.

Finally, an analysis should be made, especially with new clients, of potential conflicts of interests. While some aspects of this topic are dealt with below in more detail,[74] it deserves brief mention here. For the most part, the concerns that are involved in this inquiry bear not on securities law exposure, but on traditional questions of the propriety of a representation, and on the discomfort and potential expense of being forced to terminate a relationship.

Conflicts that may disqualify a law firm, either in its own judgment or that of the client, can take many forms, including existing representation of competitors or litigation pending against other entities involved in the transaction, or even with which the prospective client wishes to do business. A subtle potential conflict arises where the prospective client first learned about the prospective firm in a transaction with a current client of the firm. In these circumstances, the original transaction should be reviewed to ascertain whether it has any material possibility of producing litigation, since the firm's original client in the previous transaction will probably have an expectation that the firm will handle any future litigation arising out of it. If the prospective client becomes a party to such an action, the original client could be severely disappointed to find that the law firm, which had received substantial fees in the process of learning every detail of the initial transaction, was no longer available for litigation connected with that same matter.[75]

C. The Process of Evaluating Clients

As is generally true of procedures discussed in this Chapter, there is no single right or wrong method of evaluating clients. Further, because the

---

74. *See* Section VII, *infra*.

75. *See* ABA Code of Professional Responsibility, Canons 4 and 5.

objectives of evaluation to some degree depend on the extent to which the firm values long-term relationships with successful clients of good reputation, and not solely on questions of preventing errors, there is perhaps more scope for variance in these procedures than in others we discuss.

From a securities law standpoint, the principal concerns are evaluating the risk of participating in the transaction and generating adequate disclosure. While both of these interests conceivably could be dealt with at later points in the transaction, they could never be dealt with as smoothly, as objectively and with as little concern for payment for services previously rendered than at the outset. Further, careful pre-engagement evaluation of a client, together with special arrangements or discussions based on the results of that evaluation, should evidence a lack of willfulness, recklessness, or even negligence, if these become issues in litigation, particularly litigation involving inadequate disclosure about a client's background or the firm's allegedly knowing participation in an illegal transaction.

For these reasons, some form of client evaluation process appears appropriate in all securities transactions. In some settings, a standing committee of partners, charged with developing the pertinent information, is called for. This would seem to become more appropriate as the size of the firm's securities practice increases, and as the number of individual attorneys involved in that practice increases. As is often true, greater proceduralization and structure are required to achieve uniformity of practice as size increases. As a practical matter, many large firms routinely require prior review of any major new representation. This involves liability considerations as well as a review of available resources. A formalized securities-oriented evaluation process can readily be established based on this type of existing structure.

Even in settings where formal committee review of every client is impractical or otherwise not justified, use of a review committee may be highly appropriate in particular circumstances. For example, firms may wish to have a committee charged with reviewing any new securities clients who have terminated other attorneys, who have been the subject of an SEC investigation or sanctions or investor litigation, or who are proposing a venture whose success appears more uncertain than normal. Even in firms which are too small to justify such a committee, in these types of circumstances the partner proposing the representation should seek the advice of other partners knowledgeable in the securities laws.

Firms wishing to obtain the full protective benefits of a client evaluation process should evidence that process in writing. This may range from a memorandum to the file from a single responsible attorney, in circumstances in which no significant questions are raised, to formal minutes supported by extensive exhibits, in the case of committee review of a questionable representation. It should be obvious that most of the evidentiary benefit (but not necessarily the other benefits) of an evaluation process will be lost if not evidenced by a contemporaneous writing.

This discussion has focused on evaluating new clients. However, there is also merit, from the standpoints of both preventing errors and establishing a favorable evidentiary record in the case errors do occur, in having some procedure for evaluating continuing client relationships involving securities transactions. Firms may wish to consider procedures, be they required reporting of certain information to established committees, or regular communication among attorneys dealing in particular areas or with particular clients, to assure that any adverse information about a client will be available to the attorney principally charged with its securities work. Such procedures are especially important if a firm permits one partner to represent a client for which another partner refused to work for reasons related to the client's business background or prior securities transactions. While the firm may legitimately conclude that one partner is dealing with the matter too critically, the failure to develop a satisfactory record of deliberations and conclusions could result in the continued representation being interpreted as evidence of recklessness or willfulness.

Section VI

IDENTIFICATION OF SECURITIES

The failure to recognize that a security was involved in a particular transaction has been the focus of a significant amount of litigation. Most of this litigation has involved notes [76] and investment contracts,[77] but litigation has arisen even over whether something called "stock" is a security.[78] The case law, along with the complexity of this area of securities law, has generated a volume of commentary,[79] and a detailed analysis is beyond the scope of this Chapter. Moreover, the sheer volume of this case law and commentary suggests that one more treatment of the subject would not be very productive.

76. *See, e.g.,* Exchange Nat'l Bank v. Touche Ross & Co., 544 F.2d 1126 (2d Cir. 1976) (focusing on the purposes of the securities acts); Great Western Bank & Trust v. Kotz, 532 F.2d 1252 (9th Cir. 1976) (focusing on the risk capital test); McClure v. First Nat'l Bank, 497 F.2d 490, *rehearing denied* 502 F.2d 1167 (5th Cir. 1974), *cert. denied* 420 U.S. 930 (1975) (focusing on the investment-commercial dichotomy).

77. *See, e.g.,* SEC v. W. J. Howey, 328 U.S. 293 (1946); SEC v. Koscot Interplanetary, Inc., 497 F.2d 473 (5th Cir. 1974); SEC v. Glenn W. Turner Enterprises, Inc., 474 F.2d 476 (9th Cir.), *cert. denied* 414 U.S. 117 (1973).

78. *See* United Housing Foundation, Inc. v. Forman, 421 U.S. 837 (1975).

79. *E.g.,* Epstein, *Bank Participation Agreements as Securities,* 87 Banking L.J. 99 (1970); Note, *The Expanding Definition of "Security": Sale-Lease-backs and Other Commercial Leasing Arrangements,* 1972 Duke L.J. 1221; Lipton and Katz, *"Notes" Are Not Always Securities,* 30 Bus.Law 763 (1975); Pollock, *Notes Issued in Syndicated Loans—A New Test to Define Securities,* 32 Bus.Law 537 (1977); Note, *Liabilities of Lead Banks in Syndicated Loans Under the Securities Acts,* 58 B.U.L.Rev. 45–60 (1978); Note, *Overview of Promissory Notes under the Federal Securities Laws,* 6 Fordham Urb.L.J. 529–52 (1978); Note, *When is a Note a Security?,* 18 Santa Clara L.Rev. 757–78 (1978).

Protection against inadvertent failure to identify the presence of a security involves two basic elements: first, the availability of sufficient expertise to reliably determine the issue, or at least to evaluate the risk of a security being involved; and second, a method for ensuring that transactions potentially involving securities come to the attention of the attorneys possessing that expertise. The first element is a relatively simple matter, assuming that at least one attorney within the firm possesses the requisite expertise. In that case, it should be understood, possibly through a formal policy, that one or more such attorneys are to be consulted whenever there is any recognized possibility of a security being involved in a transaction. A "Catch-22" situation develops if no attorney in the firm has the requisite expertise; in that situation a firm should consider seeking advice from an independent securities specialist.

While it is easy to formulate a policy requiring particular attorneys to review particular questions, it is exceedingly difficult to develop and implement procedures that will assure that all such questions are brought to their attention. The basic requirement is that attorneys in the firm be sensitive to the possible presence of securities, and have sufficient understanding of what constitutes a security to at least recognize that a question exists. There are a variety of ways of accomplishing this, but none of them are totally reliable. One fairly formalized approach involves an effort to identify securities in the file-opening process. By including a section in the file-opening document called "identification of securities," which would include applicable federal and state definitions of a "security," [80] attorneys opening a file may be required to focus on the security issue. Another procedure for identifying securities is to require attorneys opening files, or at least those involving financial transactions, to forward a summary of facts to one of the securities law partners to determine if the transaction involves a security.

The foregoing formalized approach may be beneficial, and involve no more than a reasonable amount of effort, in some firms or with respect to particular classes of transactions. However, these procedures may not be effective in numerous other transactions in which the issue may be present. For example, in many instances the critical factual circumstances may not arise until well after the file has been opened or, with respect to an on-going client relationship, there may be a practice of utilizing sub-files rather than opening additional files for new transactions. Further, material incorporated in standard forms has a tendency to blend into the background and to be ignored, especially by the attorney who depends on his support staff to handle file-opening procedures.

Because of the difficulties of devising a formal approach that reasonably assures that all transactions possibly involving a security will be brought to the attention of a securities specialist, this is an area in which substantial reliance needs to be placed upon the training of the firm's attorneys, particularly those involved in such finance-related areas as real

80. The 1933 and 1934 Act definitions appear at 15 U.S.C. §§ 77b(1) and 78c(a)(10) (1976), respectively.

estate, tax and banking. It should be noted that, even when formal procedures are used, such training will also be important to assure that the various attorneys have a reasonable degree of understanding of the securities law definitions appearing on their file-opening documents.

For these reasons, consideration should be given to a program of conferences and/or memoranda between or from securities specialists and other attorneys, with a particular emphasis on the types of transactions in those other areas that may have securities law implications. For example, a firm's real estate attorneys should not only have a general sensitivity to the possibility of a security being involved whenever one party is using another party's funds to finance a business venture, but should also be familiar with the lines of authority involving condominiums and vacation property.[81] Similarly, attorneys involved in a banking practice should be familiar with the lines of authority involving notes.

A particular problem is presented by notes because of the inclination many attorneys have to rely on wording in both the 1933 and 1934 Acts, exempting or excepting notes and other similar documents having "a maturity at the time of issuance not exceeding nine months, exclusive of days of grace, or any renewal thereof the maturity of which is likewise limited." [82] What attorneys relying on this language must know is that the 1933 Act's exemption only applies rather narrowly to commercial paper and similar instruments, and that a number of courts have adopted contextual approaches such as the position that an *investment* instrument having a maturity of less than nine months is nonetheless subject to the 1934 Act, while a *commercial* instrument having a maturity in excess of nine months is nonetheless exempt from its coverage.[83] Thus, it can be particularly important that attorneys involved in the issuance of notes have a basic familiarity with the pertinent securities law considerations, and an understanding that these transactions may frequently require consultation with attorneys having the requisite securities law expertise.

In dealing with the problem of ensuring that initial determinations of the possible presence of a security are made, the principal source of concern is the "investment contract" concept. Unlike the other terms in the statutory definitions of a security, such as "stock" or "notes," the term "investment contract" reaches instruments and arrangements that are not routinely thought of as a security. For example, franchise arrangements, real estate time-sharing or rental pool arrangements, and discretionary commodity trading accounts have all been held to involve

---

81. *See, e.g.*, 3 H. Bloomenthal, Securities and Federal Corporate Law §§ 2.14 and 2.15 (1980 Rev.), and cases cited therein.

82. 15 U.S.C. § 77c(a)(3) sets forth the 1933 Act's exemption, and 15 U.S.C. § 78(a)(10) excepts such instruments from the 1934 Act's definition of a "security." It should be noted that the 1933 Act exemption applies to the registration provisions, and leaves one exposed to liability for inadequate disclosures.

83. *See, e.g.*, the cases cited at note 76, *supra*. For a general discussion of this area, *see* 3 H. Bloomenthal, Securities and Federal Corporate Law § 2.03 (1980 Rev.).

the sale of an investment contract.[84] While it is not possible to determine a close question on this issue without significant thought and research, it is possible to set forth the basic parameters of an investment contract in a manner sufficient for non-securities attorneys to identify the possible presence of a security.

In *SEC v. W. J. Howey Co.,*[85] the Supreme Court stated "[a]n investment contract for purposes of the Securities Act means a contract . . . whereby a person invests his money in a common enterprise and is led to expect profits solely from the efforts of the promoter or a third party. . . ."[86] This basic formulation has been repeatedly utilized, though with some modification. The Supreme Court has subsequently stated that, when analyzing any transaction, "form should be disregarded for substance and the emphasis should be on economic reality."[87] Further, in response to efforts to escape security status by pointing to some minimal efforts required on the part of the investor, the Fifth Circuit Court of Appeals has modified the "solely from the efforts of others" aspect of the *Howey* test. It has stated that the focus should be on "whether the efforts made by those other than the investor are the undeniably significant ones, those essential managerial efforts which affect the failure or success of the enterprise."[88]

It may also be helpful, as a matter of mental approach, for the firm's attorneys to be trained to inquire whether they are dealing with a transaction in which, matters of form aside, someone is investing money in a manner which serves to finance another person's business venture in which the investor has some form of continuing interest. If so, there is a reasonable chance that a security is involved.

Section VII

CONFLICTS OF INTERESTS AND INSIDE INFORMATION

In the course of discussing client selection and evaluation, we have briefly discussed the conventional concept of conflicts of interests, largely revolving around conflicting legal representations, which can arise in any transaction. In this section, we will focus on somewhat different types of conflicts which are peculiar to either representing a client in a securities transaction or investing in a client's securities. In particular, we will discuss the conflicts that arise when an attorney has relationships with a client other than as an attorney, such as an investor or a director or officer. Also, we will discuss at some length the problems of multiple representation in securities transactions.

84. *See, e.g.,* 3 H. Bloomenthal, Securities and Federal Corporate Law § 2.19 (1980 Rev.), and cases cited therein.

85. 328 U.S. 293 (1946).

86. *Id.,* at 298–99.

87. Tcherepnin v. Knight, 389 U.S. 332, 336 (1967).

88. SEC v. Koscot Interplanetary, Inc., 497 F.2d 473, 483 (5th Cir. 1974). *See also* SEC v. Glenn W. Turner Enterprises, Inc., 474 F.2d 476 (9th Cir.), *cert. denied* 414 U.S. 117 (1973).

A. Trading and Investing in Clients' Securities

The purchase and sale of the securities of a client represented in securities matters, whether for short-term trading or long-term investment, present several distinct problems that can lead to increased exposure to liability, regardless of an attorney's good intentions.

The first involves the possibility of diminished objectivity in the disclosure process. Where an attorney invests in an offering on which he is working, the investment could possibly serve as evidence he lacked willfulness in connection with a disclosure violation, based on the argument that an attorney who was aware of the problem obviously would not have made the investment. On the other hand, attorneys considering such investments should also be aware that when they make a decision to invest in a client's securities, they are making judgments about the intrinsic value of the client's securities, and are establishing a personal interest in the correctness of those judgments. The possibility for diminished objectivity, and consequent increased possibility of errors, is apparent.

In the case of an attorney's pre-existing investment in a client's securities, the potential for diminished objectivity would seem to be substantially greater, since an issuer's existing investors typically benefit from subsequent successful securities offerings. Recognizing this problem, SEC Registration Guide 56 [89] requires disclosure of "the nature and amount of any direct or indirect interest" in the issuer of an attorney named in the prospectus as having passed on legal matters. The disclosure requirement is qualified by the statement that interests of up to $30,000 per firm or $10,000 per lawyer need not be disclosed. Nonetheless, attorneys having existing investments in a securities client should be mindful that an investment of less than these amounts could have an actual impact on their objectivity with respect to critical judgment issues. In addition, even if it had no such impact, it could be damaging evidence since the issue of liability frequently involves an assessment of a defendant's mental state.

The second broad problem created by owning a client's securities is the exposure to both claims and liability based on alleged misuse of confidential or inside information, a subject recently discussed in an SEC release.[90] This can be a particularly troublesome problem for larger firms in which it is possible that information known to one attorney would be unknown but nonetheless chargeable to all other attorneys.[91] In addition,

89. SEC Securities Act Release No. 5094 (Oct. 21, 1970), 17 C.F.R. § 231.5094 (1979), [1970–71 Transfer Binder] Fed. Sec. L. Rep. (CCH) ¶ 77,917.

90. SEC Securities Exchange Act Release No. 13,437 (Apr. 8, 1977), [1977–78 Transfer Binder] Fed. Sec. L. Rep. (CCH) ¶ 81,116.

91. One of the SEC's principal concerns in *In re* Keating, Muething & Klekamp, *supra* note 64, was the failure of partners preparing securities law filings to be aware of material information known to other partners. The authors believe that for the purposes of trading restrictions the question should be actual abuse of inside information, and thus information maintained in confidence should not in that context be chargeable to other attorneys. However, there are likely in any event to be significant difficulties in establishing

if an attorney is a beneficial owner of 10% or more of a class of 1934 Act registered securities of a client, or is an officer or director, his ownership and trading in the client's securities are subject to the restrictions and strict liability rules of Section 16(b) of the 1934 Act.[92]

The third broad problem of owning a client's securities involves potential exposure to the client. It arises not under the securities laws, but rather under the ABA Code of Professional Responsibility, particularly Ethical Consideration 5–3 and Disciplinary Rule 5–101(A).[93] These provisions put attorneys on notice to take great care in analyzing whether an investment in a client's securities constitutes an impediment to the exercise of professional judgment that may adversely affect the client. The cautionary language in those provisions of the Code should be considered in the context of the possible loss of objectivity that may arise from such ownership.

Firms cannot ignore this issue, and should consider adopting one of two basic policies to deal with the problems associated with trading and investing in a client's securities: one prohibits all trading and investing in these securities, and the other permits it under certain limited circumstances. Obviously, the safest course is to prohibit all trading and investing, a policy that can be easily effectuated by adequate dissemination and maintenance of a current and readily-available list of clients. Even if a firm adopts this type of blanket prohibition, however, it would seem unnecessary to extend it to investments in mutual funds that own stock in one or more of the firm's clients. Unless a law firm has a very narrow practice, and unless a particular mutual fund invested exclusively in an industry comprised mainly of such clients, mutual fund investments are usually too remote to be of real concern, or to justify the practical difficulties of compliance with such a rule.

While a blanket prohibition may be appropriate in some law firms, others would find that it interfered with both firm business and personal objectives to an extent not justified by the increase in objectivity or reduction in exposure to claims and ultimate liability. It is not uncommon to find members of a firm who hold stock in closely-held corporations owned primarily by friends and relatives. Whether that ownership, combined with the representation of the entity, constitutes a conflict of interests can be determined on a case-by-case basis, and largely without reference to securities law problems that arise when public trading and offerings are involved. In addition, it can certainly be argued that a modest investment in a large, publicly-traded company is so insignificant that it could not cause any material decrease in objectivity or increase in exposure. In other instances, law firms may for various reasons choose to permit substantial investments in publicly-traded clients, although hopefully only after careful consideration of the attendant risks and of procedures that can reduce at least some of those risks.

---

that the trading attorney just happened to guess right and in fact was unaware of information known to other partners.

92. 15 U.S.C. § 78p(b) (1980).

93. *See also* ABA Code of Professional Responsibility, Disciplinary Rule 5–104(A).

Firms that decide not to adopt a prohibition against all trading and investments in clients' securities should devise procedures geared to the particular risks. In situations where the primary concern is with the possibility of diminished objectivity (such as securities offerings of a client which is not publicly-held), procedures should focus on a determination of whether a different attorney should be assigned to the matter. If this is not practicable or is otherwise undesirable, procedures should be adopted to ensure that other, wholly disinterested, partners are involved on a more active basis, or at a lower threshold of uncertainty as to legal and factual issues than otherwise would be the case. In cases where the attorney's services to the client do not involve offerings of securities, the concern will be focused more on the potential for abuse of inside information in the trading of securities. In either case, it would frequently be helpful to designate a particular partner or committee of partners charged with appropriate responsibilities.

When the concern is preventing trading while the firm possesses material inside information, there must be some mechanism ensuring that all existing investments in new clients, and changes in investments in existing clients, are brought to the attention of the appropriate committee or partner. When considering a proposed transaction, the partner or committee will need to consult with the partner in charge of a particular representation, and possibly other attorneys responsible for discreet areas of the representation, to determine whether the firm possesses material inside information. Frequently, it should be standard practice to encourage all sales or purchases to occur during a brief period of time following the release by the client of annual or quarterly reports; this, however, by no means provides full protection, because certain material information may have been properly withheld from the report because it was not yet ripe for disclosure or for other valid business purposes.[94]

An alternate method of dealing with possible abuse of inside information is to generally permit trading in client securities, but to combine a policy of restricting access to material information on a need-to-know basis with procedures, such as required discussions with the partner responsible for the client, for controlling purchases and sales by persons involved in the representation. Effective reliance on this approach would appear to involve two assumptions. The first is that authorities charging all members of a firm with the knowledge of any of its members would not be extended to personal investment transactions, as opposed to the reporting context in which this type of attribution has been asserted.[95] Second, this approach assumes that the procedures to preserve confidentiality are likely to be reasonably effective.

In considering procedures for maintaining confidentiality, it should be noted that attorneys have significant responsibilities to their clients in

94. *See* Financial Industrial Fund, Inc. v. McDonnell Douglas Corp., 474 F.2d 514 (10th Cir. 1973), *cert. denied* 414 U.S. 874.

95. *See supra* note 91.

this regard.[96]   Thus, procedures of this nature may be appropriate regardless of whether the firm has otherwise protected itself against securities law violations.   Determining which procedures to adopt will depend on the size and structure of the firm, and the nature of the matter.   In some instances, a policy which all personnel understand, and which prohibits the discussion of client matters except with other personnel assigned to the matter, may be sufficient.   In other circumstances, such as that of a large firm engaged to prepare a tender offer at a premium over market price, rather elaborate procedures may be called for, regardless of whether all transactions in client securities are required to be cleared by a particular partner or committee.   In such circumstances, the firm may wish to establish a set of guidelines to be followed by personnel having legitimate need for access to the information.   These guidelines could include the following:

(1)   The use of a numbering system that at least includes all documents containing confidential or sensitive information;

(2)   the assignment of each numbered document to a particular person who is responsible for the document;

(3)   the maintenance of a master list of all documents and persons having possession of the original or another numbered copy;

(4)   the utilization of code names to prevent inadvertent disclosure of sensitive names, for example, that of a target company;

(5)   a prohibition against discussing the transaction in nonprivate locations, including hallways, elevators, and generally any location not directly connected with the transaction;

(6)   stamping certain documents, after a predetermined number of copies have been made, with the words "copying prohibited";

(7)   the utilization of delivery systems for all documents so that the person receiving the documents can be specifically identified.

Even in less critical circumstances, one or more of the foregoing procedures may be appropriate, especially those that involve little inefficiency or inconvenience.   In any event, any set of such procedures in a firm representing publicly-held clients should be reinforced by a program for assuring that all personnel understand that trading on non-public information obtained in the course of the representation or, for that matter, any other use or disclosure of such information, is forbidden as a matter of both law and firm policy.

The importance of adopting guidelines to safeguard confidential information was the subject of a recent SEC release.[97]   This cautionary release focuses on information the SEC has received about situations in which law firm personnel may have abused confidential information by trading

---

96. For example, Disciplinary Rule 4–101 of the ABA Code of Professional Responsibility requires that an attorney exercise care to prevent employees from disclosing the confidences of a client.

97. SEC Securities Exchange Act Release No. 13,437 (April 8, 1977), [1977–78 Transfer Binder] Fed. Sec. L. Rep. (CCH) ¶ 81,116.

in securities before the information became public. While the release concedes that establishing procedures does not guarantee that an individual employee will not take unfair advantage of confidential information, it clearly encourages law firms to establish policies that will safeguard confidential information. In line with the release, the SEC recently obtained a settlement of charges against a patent law firm based on alleged trading by its lawyers and their acquaintances utilizing inside information about the status of a patent application the firm was handling.[98] Under the settlement, the firm agreed to adopt policies prohibiting trading in a client's securities until 48 hours after publication of material information it possesses.

The benefit of establishing such safeguards is amply demonstrated by *SEC v. Sorg Printing Co., Inc.*[99] The court in that case found that the printing company itself was not liable under Rule 10b–5 for the unlawful use by its employees of confidential information. Summary judgment was granted for the defendant company because it had taken steps to safeguard such information, had informed the SEC of the policies adopted, and had actually requested additional suggestions. The SEC had not responded to the request for additional guidelines.

In light of *Ernst & Ernst v. Hochfelder,*[100] in which the Supreme Court held that mere negligence is not sufficient to support a Rule 10b-5 cause of action, law firms can acquire substantial protection in this area by adopting policies and procedures to safeguard confidential information. The adoption and good faith enforcement of those policies should preclude a finding that the firm was willful or reckless in its handling of confidential information, even if one or more employees are held liable.

It should be understood that procedures for safeguarding client information are important, regardless of the method used to protect against abuse of that information. This is true not only as a matter of securities law compliance, but also as a matter of the attorney's responsibility to the client. Thus, the authors believe that some program to protect against the undue dissemination of client information is appropriate in all firms.

B. Serving as Director or Officer

An attorney serving as a director or officer (other than in such formal offices as assistant secretary) of a securities law client is another relationship which can increase the risk of securities law liability of a firm or the attorney. As with the ownership and trading in the client's securities, service in these capacities poses several distinct problems. One problem is the possible loss of objectivity in the disclosure process. In those circumstances, the attorney becomes in part a client, and will inevitably view the client, its past achievements, its future prospects and its management in a light other than that of an attorney responsible for assisting with

98. SEC v. Lerner, David, Littenberg & Samuel, 548 BNA Sec. Reg. & L. Rep. A-3 (Apr. 9, 1980) (D.C.D.C. Apr. 2, 1980).

99. [1974–75 Transfer Binder] Fed. Sec. L. Rep. (CCH) ¶ 95,034 (S.D.N.Y. 1975).

100. 425 U.S. 185 (1976).

securities law compliance. In addition, an attorney who serves as an officer or director is faced with a variety of conflicts of interests in discharging his duties as attorney for the entity; while most of these conflicts are present in any event, the attorney's participation as part of management clearly exacerbates them, at least in the eye of the typical beholder.

The second major problem with dual service arises in the context of registered offerings. As discussed above, Section 11 of the 1933 Act provides for liability of directors and certain officers based on material misstatements or omissions in a registration statement, subject to due diligence defenses. While *Escott v. BarChris Constr. Corp.*[101] and *Feit v. Leasco.,*[102] turned on their particular facts, they do make it rather clear that the attorney/director, because of his unique combination of professional training and insider status, faces a substantial burden in establishing the due diligence defense. As stated in *BarChris* :

> As the director most directly concerned with writing the registration statement and assuring its accuracy, more was expected of [the attorney who served as a director] in the way of reasonable investigation than could fairly be expected of a director who had no connection with the work.[103]

The authors are aware that in many circumstances clients expect their principal outside counsel to serve as a director. Moreover, it is clear that in many instances attorney/directors have made unique contributions in their service as directors, gaining influence and respect as directors that results in their legal advice being accorded greater weight by management and outside directors alike. Further, it is acknowledged that the increased understanding and familiarity with the client and its management that may be gained by service as a director can result, and in many instances has resulted, in better disclosure documents. Nonetheless, dual service does increase the securities law risks borne by the client, the firm and the particular attorney, and no such arrangement should be initiated or continued without an understanding of those risks and consideration of procedures that can ameliorate them.

Because the principal problems arising from dual service both concern the disclosure process, appropriate procedures might include placing principal responsibility for the disclosure process on an attorney who has no other affiliations with the client; to the extent this is impractical, it may be useful to institute more stringent back-up review procedures than would otherwise be utilized, and to require the dual-role attorney to seek assistance from a disinterested attorney even on questions of fact and law which involve a relatively low level of uncertainty. It may also prove useful for the dual-role attorney to be questioned concerning the client and its disclosures by an attorney who should be free to approach the matter with a greater degree of skepticism than would normally be possible in direct contacts with the client's management.

---

101. 283 F.Supp. 643, 690 (S.D.N.Y. 1968).

102. 332 F.Supp. 544 (E.D.N.Y. 1971).

103. 283 F.Supp., at 690.

Because the factual investigation process will vary widely from offering to offering, it is certain that variations on these approaches will often be appropriate. However, in designing particular approaches, it is important to keep in mind that the objectives are twofold: first, to prevent disclosure errors from occurring, despite the possible diminished objectivity of the dual-role attorney and, second, to provide a basis for successfully raising due diligence or other state-of-mind defenses in the event an error nonetheless occurs. Thus, it is essential that the procedures have both sufficient form and substance to be of practical effect and to impress a finder of fact. Obviously, a written record should be maintained. As for the expense of special disclosure procedures, to some extent the time committed to the extra procedures is likely to be offset by the time savings attributable to the dual-role attorney's familiarity with the client. To the extent this is not the case, the authors believe that the client should be aware that this is an additional cost of asking the outside attorney to serve as a director or officer.

C. Multiple Representation

This discussion is related to the prior discussion of the identification of clients; there it was suggested that the failure to properly identify clients can result in multiple representation, but without the firm realizing it. This Section, however, will deal with multiple representation in which a conscious decision has been made to represent more than one party in a securities transaction.

An instructive case, and certainly one of the more complex in this area, is *Kohn v. American Metal Climax, Inc.*[104] The facts of this case involve multiple allegations of material misrepresentations and omissions in a proxy statement concerning a merger between two related corporations. One of the alleged material omissions in the proxy statement was the failure to inform shareholders that the same law firm was advising directors of both companies regarding certain aspects of the merger.

One law firm did represent both the parent and the subsidiary company for approximately 35 years. The subsidiary was incorporated in a foreign country, and the law firm in question represented the subsidiary in negotiations with the foreign government to clear the way for the merger. The firm continued to represent the parent during these negotiations. The district court found that this created a conflict of interests that required disclosure and that the failure to disclose was a material omission. The Third Circuit reversed this specific finding, concluding it was clearly erroneous since the dual representation had ceased prior to the initiation of direct negotiations on the terms of the merger between the parent and subsidiary.[105]

While the law firm in *Kohn* was legally vindicated with respect to any conflict of interests, this was accomplished only after considerable litigation, including the district court decision that it had engaged in conduct

104. 458 F.2d 255 (3d Cir.), *cert. denied*   105. *Id.*, at 458 F.2d 268–69.
  409 U.S. 874 (1972).

that created a conflict of interests and that failure to disclose it was a material omission. Most law firms cannot endure too many such victories, and may prefer to remain somewhat farther from the line at which the conflict becomes actual rather than potential. The serious consequences of crossing that line are illustrated by a recent case concerning the sale of a construction company.

In *Hill v. Okay Constr. Co.,*[106] an attorney represented both the seller and the purchaser of a business enterprise. The seller contended that the transaction involved an outright sale, and the purchaser contended that it was a sale without recourse on the note. The attorney was named as a third-party defendant by the purchaser. While the purchaser was held liable to the seller for the purchase price, the attorney was held liable to the purchaser for the sales price and to both the seller and the purchaser for attorneys' fees and costs.

The court in *Hill* did not hold that multiple representation in the sale of the corporation was improper. Rather, it looked independently at the duties that the attorney owed to each client, as though the other client did not exist. It found that the attorney was negligent as to each client, and therefore each client was able to obtain a judgment against the attorney. The court gave absolutely no weight to any problems the attorney might have had because of the multiple representation itself.

It is also important to focus on two aspects of the ABA Code of Professional Responsibility, as adopted by most states. Disciplinary Rule 5–105(A) states that:

> A lawyer shall decline proffered employment if the exercise of his independent professional judgment in behalf of a client would be or is likely to be adversely affected by the acceptance of the proffered employment, or if it would be likely to involve him in representing *differing* interests, except to the extent permitted under DR 5–105(C) (emphasis added).

Disciplinary Rule 5–105(C) states that:

> In the situations covered by DR 5–105(A) and (B), a lawyer may represent multiple clients if it is *obvious* that he can adequately represent the interest of each and if each consents to the representation after full disclosure of the possible effect of such representation on the exercise of his independent professional judgment on behalf of each (emphasis added).

The term "differing interests" is defined in the definitional section following Canon 9 of the Code as including "every interest that will adversely affect either the judgment or the loyalty of a lawyer to a client, whether it be a conflicting, inconsistent, diverse, or other interest." This definition tends to blur any distinction between the two central prohibitions in Disciplinary Rule 5–105(A); however, it does clarify the basis for declining multiple representation and leaves no doubt that something short of an actual conflict of interests will prohibit the acceptance of such

106. 312 Minn. 324, 252 N.W.2d 107 (1977).

representation.　The Code also attempts to solve the problem of close questions by using the word "obvious" in Disciplinary Rule 5–105(C). However, that may be the most ignored word in the entire Code.

In the securities area, multiple representation poses problems beyond those of exposure to one or both of the clients, or to violations of the Code.　The problems in this context include potentially diminished objectivity, and thus increased risk of disclosure errors, and increased difficulty of establishing a due diligence or other state-of-mind defense.　As a practical matter, it is virtually inconceivable that one firm would act as counsel to clearly distinct clients, such as issuer and underwriter, in a major securities transaction.　However, dual representation in more modest transactions, or of related parties in many transactions, is probably not unusual.　The *Hill* case, above, is an example of the type of circumstances which, if the sale of a block of stock had been involved, could have resulted in securities law problems.　In these types of situations, the conflict is so direct that a firm should accept the dual representation only: (1) in unusual circumstances; (2) with the express approval of both the clients and a group of partners charged with considering the matter; (3) with each client's full understanding that all information material to the purchase or sale learned from one client and adverse to the interests of the other must be disclosed to the other; and (4) in connection with a well-documented effort to assure that all such information of which the firm has knowledge or notice is made available to each client.

Perhaps more typical would be circumstances in which the same law firm prepares documentation for an offering of a client's securities and also advises its principal officers on such matters as employment contracts, fringe benefits, or transactions between the issuer and another company controlled by an officer.　With respect to these types of transactions, it should be recognized that the multiple representation may both place the firm on notice of additional factual information, and also raise the possibility of diminished objectivity in disclosure matters.　For these reasons, this type of representation of secondarily-interested parties should normally be undertaken only with the understanding that the primary duty is to the issuer, and only in conjunction with procedures to assure that objectivity is maintained and that the firm meets, and can prove that it has met, the standards for applicable state-of-mind defenses. Among appropriate measures would be back-up review of matters related to the secondary representation by an attorney not involved with it, required consultation among at least two partners with respect to disclosure of matters related to the secondary representation, and careful and thorough documentation of the basis for any decisions against disclosure of information with respect to the secondary client.

Section VIII

LEGAL OPINIONS

Legal opinions in securities transactions can arise in a variety of contexts and deal with a variety of subject matters, including the following: due and valid issuance of securities in public offerings; private placements of securities; acquisitions and dispositions of securities; audit letters; debt financing and bond issues; and tax and title matters. Requests for opinions in these and other areas usually arise out of a specific requirement of the securities laws or a specific requirement of the transaction itself. In either event, issuance of the opinion involves perhaps the epitome of the formalized private legal process. It calls for a structured approach in compliance with firm policies and procedures; indeed, it is the expectation of just this careful, structured and considered approach that, in the view of many attorneys, distinguishes a client's request for an opinion from a request for less formal "advice."

Because of the client's expectations and the formal nature of an opinion, the potential for exposure to liability for errors is substantial. It is even greater when the opinion is rendered in and is an essential element of a securities transaction in which parties other than the client have both significant interests and a variety of potential avenues of legal recourse. For these reasons, firm policies and procedures for opinions in security transactions should often include such precautionary measures as (1) engagement letters, (2) preparation and preservation of a written record, (3) appropriate investigation of the facts, including consideration of the reasons why reliance is placed on those facts, (4) a formal review procedure, and (5) a careful recitation in the opinion of all restrictions on its use.

In the following discussion of these measures, we are not seeking to deal at all with the meaning of various statements frequently contained in opinion letters, and for the most part we do not deal with the nature of opinions that an attorney may render. These are important topics with which lawyers rendering opinions in securities matters should be thoroughly familiar, but we refer the reader to excellent treatments of those particular topics,[107] and also of the specialized terminology and procedures applicable to audit letter responses.[108] For the purposes of our discussion, we assume that an attorney is conversant with the analysis called for by and the expression utilized in opinions, and deal instead with questions of how to proceed to render the opinion in a manner that minimizes the risk of error or consequent liability.

A. The Engagement Letter and Limitations on the Opinion

The engagement letter finds one of its most important uses in the area of legal opinions, for two principal reasons. First, it assures prior understanding with respect to critical parameters of the opinion, including its scope, the parties who may rely on it, and the factual information

107. In particular, *see* Assoc. of the Bar of the City of New York, *Report by Special Committee on Lawyers' Role in Securities Transactions,* 32 Bus. Law. 1879 (1979), and Committees of the New York County Lawyers Association, the Association of the Bar of the City of New York, and the New York State Bar Association, *Legal Opinions to Third Parties: An Easier Path,* 34 Bus. Law. 1891 (1979).

108. *See* Stephen L. Wells, *How to Respond to an Auditor's Request for Information,* 25 Prac. Law., Dec. 1979, p. 39.

that must be made available to support the opinion. While limitations of this nature would frequently appear in the opinion letter itself, they should be clarified at the outset, to prevent misunderstandings that may otherwise become apparent only at closing. If the client is unwilling to agree to the specified limitations, then the advisability of undertaking the representation should be questioned.

The failure to specify limitations regarding parties and time parameters has contributed to litigation against attorneys arising from their opinion letters.[109] If the limitations are not set forth in the opinion letter itself, it is unlikely that asserted limitations privately agreed upon between the attorney and client will insulate the attorney from liability.[110] In this regard, Guideline One of Part II of the Report of the Special Committee on the Lawyer's Role in Securities Transactions [111] should be followed. It states:

> Before rendering an opinion, a lawyer should ascertain the purpose for which the opinion is sought; whether the opinion is to be addressed to the client or another recipient; whether any persons other than the client or other addressee are intended to be entitled to rely on the opinion and, if so, their identity; and whether use by and reliance on the opinion should be expressly limited to a specific person or group of persons or to a particular purpose. When a securities law opinion is to be limited to any particular person or purpose, it will usually be advisable for such limitation to be clearly stated in the opinion.

The second reason that the engagement letter may serve an important role with respect to opinion letters is that it is an appropriate vehicle for specifying the persons who bear responsibility for various aspects of the work required to complete the opinion, and also for providing the client with general information about the attorney's role. Depending on the nature of the opinion, it may be appropriate to specify who is responsible for gathering factual information, as well as any back-up material that may be required before the firm will rely upon factual matters presented to it by the client. Particularly in circumstances where the client is either responsible for gathering a significant amount of factual information or will be comparing its own factual circumstances against hypothetical facts supplied to the attorney, it is important that the engagement letter, as well as later communications, be carefully phrased to prevent misunderstandings about the pertinent facts.[112]

If the transaction concerns unregistered securities, the engagement letter could include a copy of ABA Formal Opinion 335,[113] to assure that the client understands the limits on the attorney's duties of inquiry into

---

109. *See, e. g.,* Roberts v. Ball, Hunt, Hart, Brown & Baerwitz, 57 Cal.App.3d 104, 128 Cal.Rptr. 901 (1976).

110. *See* SEC v. Spectrum, Ltd., 489 F.2d 535 (2d Cir. 1973); Escott v. Bar-Chris Constr. Corp., 283 F.Supp. 643 (S.D.N.Y. 1968).

111. *Report by Special Committee, supra* note 107, at 1886–87.

112. ABA Comm. on Professional Ethics, Opinions No. 335 (1974).

113. *Id.*

factual matters presented by the client. This Formal Opinion indicates that attorneys have important duties in this area, but that these duties stop well short of a general requirement of a "factual audit" of the client's affairs.

If the client has indicated an interest in an opinion that depends on factual determinations going beyond those an attorney is qualified to make, such as may frequently be true of opinions concerning compliance with the Rule 146 exemption, it may be helpful to clarify the attorney's role by specific mention of certain SEC releases set forth or mentioned in Formal Opinion 335. In circumstances suggesting that there may be pressure to go beyond the attorney's appropriate role, it might also be beneficial to attach those releases to the engagement letter. For example, the client's attention could be drawn to Securities Act Releases Nos. 4445 [114] and 5168.[115] In those releases, it is stated:

> Indeed, if an attorney furnishes an opinion based solely upon hypothetical facts which he has made no effort to verify, and if he knows that his opinion will be relied upon as a basis for a substantial distribution of unregistered securities, a serious question arises as to the propriety of his professional conduct.

Reference could also appropriately be made in the engagement letter to certain portions of the Report of the Special Committee on the Lawyer's Role in Securities Transactions. For example, such reference might be appropriate if the client proposed that the attorney rely on information that by its nature cannot be verified and thus "may be erroneous or incomplete in a material respect." [116]

B. Factual Investigation

A thorough treatment of the nature and extent of factual inquiry appropriate for a particular opinion are beyond the scope of this Chapter. However, several comments of a general nature are in order. First, the objectives of factual investigation are twofold. One is to build the necessary predicate for reaching the conclusions set forth in the opinion. The other is to have a reasonable basis for concluding the opinion is to be used for a proper purpose, or at least that the attorney has no reason to suspect it is being used for an illegal purpose. The latter objective is normally not a problem when the attorney is representing the client with respect to the entire transaction, but may merit specific attention when an attorney is asked to render an opinion on a narrow point and is not otherwise involved in the transaction.[117]

114. SEC Securities Act Release No. 4445 (Securities Exchange Act Release No. 6721) (Feb. 2, 1962), 17 C.F.R. § 241.6721 (§ 231.445) (1978), 2 Fed. Sec. L. Rep. (CCH) at ¶¶ 22,753–59.

115. SEC Securities Act Release No. 5168 (Securities Exchange Act Release No. 9239) (July 7, 1971); 2 Fed. Sec. L. Rep. (CCH) ¶ 22,760.

116. *Report by Special Committee, supra* note 107, at 1888 (Part II, Guideline 4(a)).

117. *See* SEC v. Spectrum, Ltd., 489 F.2d 535 (2d Cir. 1973).

Second, the extent to which it is appropriate to rely on facts provided by the client, or on hypothetical facts posed by the client, will be significantly affected by both the attorney's experience with the client and the degree to which persons other than the client will rely on or be affected by the opinion. Where there is a long-standing relationship in which the client has proven to be candid and accurate in discussing factual matters, the attorney could engage in relatively less independent review than might otherwise be required. For example, this situation might arise in considering the financial capacity of a corporate general partner in connection with an opinion on whether a limited partnership would be taxed as a partnership. Similarly, if the opinion has little effect on third parties, as might be the case when the client seeks an opinion on consequences to it of assuming obligations under a merger candidate's pension plans, heavy reliance could be placed on facts supplied by the client, even though the opinion is to be delivered to the client in connection with the closing of a securities transaction. On the other hand, an opinion concerning the exempt status of a proposed offering, while intended for primary reliance by the client, has a substantial effect on the purchasers and also relates directly to a major source of liability exposure; thus, a significant amount of independent review is more likely to be appropriate.

Third, in almost no circumstance would it be appropriate to rely on a client's description or inspection of documents from which legal conclusions are drawn, such as corporate articles, by-laws or resolutions. While it may be appropriate to rely on the client's certification that the attorney has been provided true and correct copies of such documents, even where the only party in interest is the client the attorney is the person responsible for determining the legal effects of such documents, and can ordinarily do so only after actual inspection.

Finally, while there is no clear formulation of when an attorney's duty to inquire into factual matters ends, there is agreement that this duty continues for at least so long as the facts are materially incomplete, suspect or inconsistent.[118] This would seem to be true even where the client alone is directly affected by the opinion, in part as a matter of protecting against liability to the client, and in part to develop adequate assurance that the opinion is not being used in an illegal transaction. Because of the imprecision of these concepts, and the extent to which they involve matters of judgment, when questions of this nature arise they should ordinarily be addressed directly, and a determination that additional inquiry is not required should be approved by at least one partner other than the one principally responsible for the representation.

---

118. *See Report by Special Committee, supra* note 107, at 1894–96 (Part II, Guideline 4); *Formal Opinion No. 335, supra* note 112, at 478; Landau, *Legal Opinions Rendered in Securities Transactions, supra* note 40, at 20–25. *See also* SEC v. Cohen, [Current Binder] Fed. Sec. L. Rep. (CCH) ¶ 97,335 (D.C. D.C. Apr. 2, 1980) (attorneys agree to have a "reasonable basis" for relying upon facts bearing on tax opinions in limited partnership offerings).

C. **Preparation and Preservation of a Written Record**

While careful investigation and preparation of an opinion letter may significantly reduce the likelihood of error, much of the evidentiary benefit of that careful process will be lost unless preserved in a written record. Indeed, there is little reason for not reducing to writing the methods and procedures used to investigate the factual and legal matters that are involved in the issuance of an opinion, other than time and expense, which are of course involved with any preventative procedure. Even in circumstances when the various inquiries and procedures are not fully elaborated in writing, certain points are particularly important.

When back-up legal research is not set forth in the opinion, memoranda should be prepared. Not only is the mental discipline inherent in the writing process important to reaching an appropriate legal conclusion, but an attorney unable to show the bases of legal conclusions would find it difficult to meet a negligence standard (which would probably be applicable in an action by the client).

Where significant reliance is placed on the client's factual representations, the basis for this approach should be reflected; in some circumstances, such as when a client has been represented in various matters by a number of the firm's attorneys, it could be useful to include formal responses from each such attorney concerning their experiences with the client's candor and reliability. Where significant facts involved in the opinion are subject to change, such as the status of litigation or an applicable usury rate that floats with market interest rates, the record should reflect the measures taken to ensure accuracy at the time the opinion was delivered. Where there have been disagreements about legal and factual matters, the parties involved and the rationale for the ultimate resolution should be recorded, especially where the decision is against either further inquiry or qualification of the opinion. Even in the absence of disagreements, the rationale for determining that particular factors or legal issues are not pertinent, or that the duty of inquiry has been met, should be recorded.

The persons making such decisions should routinely be identified. In the case of lengthy or complex opinions, especially where a number of attorneys are involved in its preparation, it is a sound practice to prepare at an early stage an outline of the work to be performed by the various participants; if the client has significant responsibilities in the process, it should receive a copy with the engagement letter. In any event, the outline should be included in the written record.

Obviously, judgments must be made about the nature and extent of the written record that should be prepared in a given situation. Perhaps with some justification, attorneys feel an unwillingness to record their thoughts and actions for use in possible future litigation, because of the uncertainty of how particular information could be used in an unanticipated context. This concern, however, must be weighed against the known risk of potential litigation involving particular decisions and judgments, and the known benefit of being able to establish that, right or wrong, the attorney approached the representation in a non-reckless, non-willful or non-negligent manner. The authors believe that a more complete record is likely to be more effective for this purpose.

The written back-up should be organized, perhaps according to an annotated copy of the opinion letter or to the outline of the work to be done. Organization is important not only to make the material readily-accessible in the future, but also to reduce the likelihood of overlooking important points. The written back-up should be prepared with a view towards the possibility of disputes or litigation, recognizing that laymen may be listening to testimony based upon these memoranda, or at least to the testimony of expert witnesses who have reviewed the memoranda.

D. Firm Review of Opinions

Within the process of issuing an opinion letter, there will be reviews of factual and legal matters by the partner in charge of issuing the opinion; however, it is suggested that at least one independent partner not directly connected with the transaction be required to review and approve the opinion before it is issued. This is the equivalent of the "cold review" sometimes used in the preparation of disclosure documents, which is discussed below. It is more beneficial with opinion letters because, as a rule, they are more narrowly focused and enable the reader to form a judgment without as much detailed background concerning the client. This is in part due to the nature of the opinion letter itself, which should either set forth all the facts and law upon which it is based, or be accompanied by back-up memoranda and factual abstracts.

E. Subsequent Review of Opinions

The engagement letter should inform the client of, and the opinion itself should set forth, whatever limitations are appropriate concerning the opinion's scope and purpose, and the time within which it may be utilized. In the case of opinions relating to transactions of a continuing nature, it may be appropriate to refer in the opinion to any perceived likelihood that facts or law may change in a manner impairing its validity. Even if this is done, however, a procedure should be instituted to periodically review opinions relating to continuing transactions to determine whether there are any events that would compel the firm to inform the client or other persons entitled to rely upon the opinion that, notwithstanding any previous analysis, the opinion is no longer accurate and can no longer be relied upon.[119]

119. With regard to duties to correct prior statements that have become misleading, *see SEC v. Manor Nursing Centers, Inc.,* 458 F.2d 1082 (2d Cir. 1972) (failure to correct misleading prospectus; attorney among enjoined defendants); *Fischer v. Kletz,* 266 F.Supp. 180 (S.D.N.Y. 1967) (failure of accountants to correct certificate upon subsequent discovery of misstatements in the certified financial statements); Parker, Attorney Liability Under the Securities Laws after *Ernst & Ernst v. Hochfelder,* 10 Loyola L. Rev. 521 (1977).

F. Utilizing Special Counsel

In certain situations, in order to render the opinion requested by the client, it is necessary to obtain opinions from local counsel in various states. In selecting local counsel, care must be taken to ensure that the local counsel is well qualified in the particular area of law. Negligence in the selection of local counsel does provide a basis for a cause of action against the attorney selecting local counsel.[120] In addition, even if an ultimate defense exists based upon the lack of negligence of the firm seeking the opinion of local counsel, there is obviously nothing to be gained from associating unqualified local counsel.

Section IX

DISCLOSURE DOCUMENTS

This Section will deal with procedures that can be implemented to reduce the likelihood of errors in the preparation of various disclosure documents. As a matter of convenience, the prospectus will be the focus of attention. However, the following procedures are also generally relevant in the preparation of other disclosure documents, such as periodic reports and proxy materials. Some of these procedures are suggested based upon their inclusion in the SEC settlements that were previously discussed,[121] while others are generally sound practices that will reduce the likelihood of error, provide a basis for defenses should error nonetheless occur, or both.

A. Engagement Letters

Engagement letters should routinely be prepared in connection with representing clients who seek the review or preparation of disclosure documents. The payment of fees and expenses should of course be covered in this engagement letter. Aside from its importance as a business matter, fee arrangements can be of some consequence in the disclosure process. In particular, arrangements under which all or a substantial portion of the attorney's compensation is contingent upon the closing of the transaction can create a serious source of diminished objectivity as the scheduled closing approaches. Moreover, such arrangements can lay the foundation for allegations of willfulness or recklessness. This problem also exists, although to a significantly lesser degree, where payment is deferred until closing, or where a premium is due if based on the closing. Also, the right of withdrawal in the case of disclosure disagreements, discussed below, could be seriously affected if it is not understood that fees earned through the date of a proper withdrawal are payable by the client.

120. *See* Tormo v. Yormark, 398 F.Supp. 121. *See* Section IV, *supra*.
      1159 (D.N.J. 1975).

The engagement letter should also define the scope of the attorney's undertaking, including matters relating to any opinion letters, as discussed above. In addition, it should generally define the responsibilities assigned to the client and to other professionals; while the specifics of the respective duties can be refined at later points in the process, general agreement is important at the outset to prevent misunderstandings that could jeopardize the representation or transaction. Either in the engagement letter, or as soon thereafter as feasible, a schedule should be prepared setting forth each major category of work that must be completed, the date it should be completed, and the person or entity responsible for it. Cover letters or other evidence of delivery of the schedule to each responsible person or entity should be preserved, and a written acknowledgment could be required in order to eliminate future disagreement over whether the assignment was accepted. For assignments made to the firm itself, it is not necessary to specify in the engagement letter or schedule which attorneys will undertake specific duties, but such assignments should be made in writing within the firm.

Clarification of the respective roles in the engagement letter serves several purposes. It helps eliminate disputes with the client over the tasks an attorney has agreed to perform. Also, together with the schedule of major tasks, it helps prevent the occurrence of errors by forcing an attorney to focus in an orderly manner on the steps needed to complete the transaction and by establishing a framework for a smoothly orchestrated effort. Finally, it can reduce the likelihood of liability by defining the scope of the attorney's inquiry, and by providing both an occasion for formulating and a method of stating conclusions as to why particular matters are not within the scope of his responsibilities.

The engagement letter is also the appropriate method of setting forth provisions for withdrawal, especially based on disagreements over disclosure. While withdrawal is not a topic that is easily discussed with clients, it is nonetheless relatively easier to discuss in the abstract prior to embarking on a representation than it is with only a few days left to file a registration statement. Although this may be obvious, it would also be prudent for the engagement letter to point out that withdrawal near the date a transaction must be completed could jeopardize its closing. The importance of withdrawal provisions is that without them the attorney could be placed in the unpleasant position of being unable to withdraw from what he believes may be an illegal transaction, without exposure to the client (at least if the transaction were established to have been legal), or without any understanding with respect to payment for what could be a large amount of services. The same is generally true for withdrawal based on a conflict of interests, which might also be discussed in the engagement letter; however, the attorney will bear a much greater burden in this area because conflicts usually can and should be evaluated prior to undertaking the representation.

In framing the language of the withdrawal provisions in an engagement letter, one should not attempt to insulate the law firm from liability to the client. That is, a distinction must be made between the disclosure of the possibility of withdrawal under proper circumstances and any promise by the client that it will take no action in the event of an improper withdrawal. In this regard, Canon 6 of the ABA Code of Professional Responsibility, adopted in a nearly identical form by most states, prohibits attorneys from insulating themselves against liability to their clients. The disclosure in the engagement letter will, however, serve to insulate the attorneys from liability in the case of a proper withdrawal, since the client would be generally unable to prevail on a cause of action for breach of contract to perform agreed services or for negligence in failing to reveal the possibility of withdrawal or its consequences.

An engagement letter recently used by one of the authors in connection with a proposed Regulation A offering is attached as Appendix A. In keeping with the authors' view of the various policies and procedures discussed in this Chapter, as explained in the Introduction, the letter does not incorporate all of the foregoing recommendations. Rather, it reflects an evaluation of the particular transaction and client, and a judgment that some matters could more appropriately be handled in subsequent correspondence, or did not present a material risk in the particular context.

B. References to Counsel in Disclosure Documents

As a general rule, exposure to liability is increased, from several possible sources, when an attorney is named in a disclosure document. One source is Section 11 of the 1933 Act, which imposes liability as an expert only on parties named as such with their consent. Another practical source of increased exposure is the simple fact that higher visibility attracts more attention. Finally, one fairly recent case deserves discussion. In *Black & Co. v. Nova-Tech*,[122] a federal district court held that, under the Oregon blue sky laws, the designation of a law firm as corporate counsel in an annual report to shareholders was sufficient, for the purpose of a motion to quash service and dismiss, to make the law firm's partners participants in any unlawful transaction in which the annual report was used for promotional purposes. Although the court specifically pointed out that its decision did not involve the issue of ultimate liability, the expense of a further defense in such actions alone suggests the need for caution in this area.

Designation as corporate counsel in annual reports involves an element of prestige and, to use a controversial word, advertising. In addition, this form of advertising is free, traditionally has not been the subject of any criticism from disciplinary agencies, and may be insisted upon by clients who are proud of their attorneys. These benefits are not to be ignored but, as demonstrated by *Black*, they carry with them certain exposure, at least where the client is likely to use the report not merely for communicating with shareholders, but also for promoting transactions with other parties. Sensitivity to the potential risks may become somewhat greater

---

122. 333 F.Supp. 468 (D.Or. 1971).

if the SEC follows through on its proposal for a disclosure system that integrates the filings required under the 1933 and 1934 Acts. At present, it is proposing that the annual report to shareholders be the primary document in this system, at least with respect to certain large issuers, with the result that it would be distributed to prospective securities purchasers.[123]

A prospectus for a registered offering will normally contain a section headed "Legal Matters" or some similar phrase, stating that named law firms have passed on certain legal matters. A random sampling of prospectuses suggests that in recent years the description of the matters passed upon has narrowed. One now rarely sees statements such as "Certain legal matters in connection with the offering have been passed upon by . . . ." Rather, the language is now more likely to be "The legality of the securities being offered hereby . . . ," or even more narrowly, "The validity of the securities being offered hereby . . . ." The latter formulations are clearly preferable. The opinion required by the registration forms extends only to the "legality" of the securities, with specific reference required to whether they will be "legally issued, fully paid and non-assessable, and, if debt securities, whether they will be binding obligations . . . ."[124] The term "validity" is preferable to the term "legality" in the summary description, because it avoids the suggestion that a firm has passed upon all matters that may affect the legality of the offering. It might be noted that the underwriters' counsel is normally named as also passing on the securities, but such counsel need not file a written consent to being named and thus, unlike the registrant's counsel, is not exposed to Section 11 expert's liability.[125]

Other than the foregoing, and occasional requirements of specialized registration forms[126] and the SEC Staff with respect to tax matters, there is little reason or occasion for attorneys to be named in disclosure documents, including the periodic reports and proxy statements. In any event, no attorney should ever be named as having reviewed a disclosure document on behalf of a client. It is one thing to assist a client with its disclosure obligations, but quite another to publicly vouch for the disclosure document, especially in the absence of the type of elaborate standardized procedures that define the obligations of, and thus protect, accountants who are named as having audited or performed other services with respect to financial statements.[127]

---

123. *See* SEC Securities Act Release Nos. 6176–79 (Jan. 15, 1980).

124. *See* Form S-1, Instructions to Exhibit 6, 2 Fed. Sec. L. Rep. (CCH) ¶ 7,128.

125. *See* SEC Registration Guide 38, SEC Securities Act Release No. 5094 (October 21, 1970), 17 C.F.R. § 231.5094 (1979), [1970–71 Transfer Binder] Fed. Sec. L. Rep. (CCH) ¶ 77,917, and 1933 Act Section 11(a)(4), 15 U.S.C. § 77k(a)(4) (1976).

126. *See* Form S-11, Instructions to Exhibit 6(a), 2 Fed. Sec. L. Rep. (CCH) ¶ 7,239.

127. The risks of endorsing, or appearing to endorse, an issue of securities are amply illustrated in *Katz v. Amos Treat & Co.*, 411 F.2d 1046 (2d Cir. 1969), in which an attorney's encouraging oral responses to an investor's inquiries resulted in a jury question on his liability under Section 12(2) of the 1933 Act as a participant in the offering.

C. The Factual Inquiry and Legal Requirements

1. *Introduction*

The information set forth in a disclosure document is presented by the issuer, not the attorney, and is not audited or otherwise vouched for by an attorney. Nonetheless, an attorney does advise the client on the type of information that must be included, and assists with judgments about materiality. He also assists in drafting the document with the goal that it "says what the lawyer understands the issuer intends it to say, is unambiguous, and is written in a way that is designed to protect the issuer from later claims of overstatement, misleading implications, omissions or other deficiencies due to the manner in which the statements in question have been written." [128]

An attorney is not privileged to overlook information that gives him reason to believe that statements are incomplete or inaccurate. Also, the client, which is most directly exposed to liability for misstatements or omissions, normally expects an attorney to apply his experience and expertise in a good faith effort to produce an accurate and complete disclosure document. Moreover, it is not uncommon for underwriters to require that the issuer's counsel include statements in an opinion letter concerning their belief in the accuracy of particular portions of disclosure documents, or at least their absence of belief in the inaccuracy or incompleteness of such documents. For all of these reasons, in normal practice an attorney has a very important role in the preparation of disclosure documents and the process of developing and testing the factual materials included in them.

The procedures discussed below are not intended to reflect the authors' judgments with respect to the minimum role in the factual inquiry process that an attorney may play. Rather, like most policies and procedures set forth in this Chapter, they represent suggestions of steps that attorneys can take, often with the cooperation of their clients, to decrease the likelihood of material misstatements or omissions, and to increase the likelihood that applicable due diligence or other state-of-mind defenses will be available to both an attorney and the client. Whether the client's refusal to cooperate with one or more of these procedures would increase the exposure to liability to an unacceptable level is a different question that goes beyond the scope of this Chapter, and must be determined on a case-by-case basis.

The area of factual inquiry is perhaps less amenable to effective standardized procedures than any other portion of the securities transaction process. The variables are almost endless, the subject matter may involve technical and business concepts with which an attorney is not trained to deal, and seemingly straightforward facts may acquire entirely different significance if coupled with other facts which may or may not come to an attorney's attention. For these reasons, emphasis should be

---

128. *See Report by Special Committee,*
supra note 107, at 1888 (Part III, Guideline 5).

placed on the training and background of the attorneys charged with assisting in the disclosure process, a matter to be discussed below, and also on their adopting a somewhat cautious, skeptical attitude not only towards particular items of information, but also while engaging in a general inquiry about the issuer.

In considering the appropriateness of playing a probing, skeptical role, it should be remembered that other participants in the process are unlikely to play that role. Officers and other principals of issuers can normally be expected to focus on the positive aspects of the company, and unlike the attorney they do not spend their professional lives either anticipating the ways in which things can go wrong, or litigating the consequences when they do. While the future holds myriad possibilities that can never be wholly anticipated, it is better to consciously explore those possible sources of difficulty that can be identified, and to include reference in the disclosure document to those that are regarded as material, than to be totally at the mercy of a fact-finder's subsequent determination of whether particular events should have been anticipated.

2. *Particular Procedures*

The most important aspects of an effective factual inquiry are probably an attorney's mental approach, background and perhaps even luck in asking the right questions or making the right connections. However, there are particular procedures which are frequently employed and which do increase the reliability of the process.

For one, an attorney should generally discuss the issuer and its prospects with its officers, probing into such matters as management experience, training and track record, competition, changing market patterns, price trends, effect of broad economic trends, raw material and labor needs, technological developments, the recent experiences of similar entities, actual or potential related-party transactions, and future capital needs and possible impact on current investors of meeting those needs. Where this questioning leads depends wholly on the attorney and his or her evaluation of the responses. In any event, in this process, an attorney will call upon his or her experience in similar or related matters, in the ways in which business enterprises can encounter financial difficulties, and in the types of disclosure problems that have led to litigation. One approach to this process that some attorneys may find helpful is to consciously ask, first, "How can this go wrong?" and, second, "What would I ask if I was representing an investor who lost money in this offering?"

On a somewhat more specific level, a questionnaire should normally be directed to all officers and directors regarding disclosure items about which they as individuals would have particular knowledge, such as their compensation and stock ownership, their transactions with the issuer, and their background and experience. While much of this information may be obtainable through company records, requiring that it also be supplied by individuals provides a useful check, may reveal information that has been overlooked, and generally provides a more reliable factual basis. An example of such a questionnaire, keyed to the requirements of a fully registered offering in effect in the Fall of 1979, is attached as Appendix B.

In the course of preparing to issue an opinion letter with respect to the valid issuance of securities, an attorney would normally undertake a review of governing statutes, the corporate charter, by-laws, and director and shareholder action. In the case of an initial offering, this would normally be a rather extensive review. Whether or not rendering an opinion, an attorney normally should review these materials, focusing not only on actions directly relating to the issuance of the securities, but also on other matters that could affect an investor. Examples are outstanding preemptive rights from earlier offerings, options and employment contracts, shareholder buy-sell agreements to which the corporation is a party, and any discussions of business plans and prospects. In reviewing the official corporate records, it may be well to keep in mind that they would be readily discoverable in subsequent litigation with a disgruntled investor.[129]

Disclosure documents frequently contain descriptions in varying detail of such documents as contracts with major suppliers or customers, employment contracts, credit agreements, underwriting agreements and documents defining the rights of security holders. An attorney should routinely review documents described or referenced in a disclosure document. While an attorney does not have professional expertise in evaluating business and technical information, he should have professional expertise in determining the contents and legal effect of legal documents.

Where a firm represents a client in a variety of matters, involving a number of its attorneys, care should be taken to assure that material information possessed by any of the attorneys is brought to the attention of the partner responsible for the disclosure document. A recent Rule 2(e) proceeding involved precisely this point, and the settlement included the firm's undertaking to establish procedures (the details of which were not specified) designed to assure "that the knowledge of the members of the firm was communicated to the persons responsible for preparing disclosure documents so that adequate disclosure of material information—which was within the firm's knowledge—was made."[130] The authors suggest that all attorneys involved in representing the client could be required to respond to a written inquiry concerning their knowledge of material transactions or uncertainties, perhaps with a particular emphasis on such sensitive areas as insider transactions and violations of law.[131] In addition, the partners responsible for the principal areas of representation could be required to review pertinent portions of the proposed disclosure document.

129. *Cf. Garner v. Wolfinbarger,* 430 F.2d 1093 (5th Cir. 1970), *cert. denied* 401 U.S. 974 (1971).

130. *In re* Keating, Muething & Klekamp, SEC Securities Exchange Act Release No. 15982 (July 2, 1979), 511 Sec. Reg. L. Rep. (BNA) E-1, E-6 (July 11, 1979).

131. *See In re* United States Steel Corp., SEC Securities Exchange Act Release No. 16,233 (Sep. 27, 1979), 522 Sec. Reg. L. Rep. (BNA) G-1 (October 3, 1979), concerning disclosures of violations of environmental regulations.

When assisting in the assembly of information into the disclosure document, it will often be appropriate for an attorney to obtain and review back-up schedules from the client's officers and employees who compile the information. Where, for example, it is contemplated that the disclosure document will state there have been a certain number of loans, aggregating a certain dollar amount, to a particular related party over a specified period of time, a work sheet itemizing each loan should be prepared. This will permit the attorney to check the information for consistency, and also to determine whether there has been an error in communication between him and the person compiling the information. For clients that must prepare or update a disclosure document on a regular basis, such schedules will also prove to be a useful guide in determining which transactions no longer, by virtue of the passage of time, need be disclosed.

Disclosure requirements under the federal securities laws have undergone rapid changes in recent years, particularly in the areas of management remuneration and disclosure of securities ownership. Also, the promulgation of Regulation S-K has resulted in greater uniformity among the various federal disclosure documents, but in the process has resulted in modifications. Similarly, the disclosure requirements applicable to Rule 146 offerings have been modified in recent years, by a specific provision applicable to offerings of less than $1,500,000. Moreover, the SEC is now actively considering a major realignment of the nature and roles of periodic reports and documents for use in securities offerings,[132] and is embarked on a continuing experiment with the types of disclosure appropriate for small businesses. Clearly, care must be taken to assure that current disclosure standards and other legal requirements are being followed. This frequently involves review of a current version of the applicable rules, regulations and forms during the course of each offering.

An obvious but sometimes overlooked guide in the consideration of factual information is the particular disclosure regulation or form applicable to the specific transaction. It might be noted that careful, point-by-point consideration of each specified requirement is particularly important in exempt transactions, which will not be reviewed by the SEC and which could fail to qualify for the exemption as a result of a disclosure inadequacy. For example, Rule 146 requires, as a condition of the exemption, that investors receive the type of information they would receive in a registered offering, subject to certain qualifications and specific methods of complying with the requirement. Similarly, Rule 242 requires that non-accredited investors receive the same kind of information that would be included in a Form S-18 prospectus, subject to a materiality exception.

A significant source of information and insight about an issuer is its independent accountants. In discharging their responsibilities under generally accepted auditing standards, they will normally make a rather

---

132. *See supra* note 123 and the accompanying discussion, and SEC Securities Act Release No. 6176–79 (Jan. 15, 1980).

extensive review of the company's books and records, including such non-financial documents as important contracts and the corporate minute book. While in some ways duplicative of the attorney's review, the accountants' perspective and objectives are somewhat different, and can bring additional important considerations to light. Even in offerings that are not underwritten, and that thus may not include a "comfort letter," [133] the accountants will normally not give their consent to inclusion of their certificate without having reviewed the textual portion of the disclosure document to ascertain its consistency with the financial statements and notes. Attorneys should not overlook the opportunity to discuss with the accountants any problems they have encountered, and their views on disclosure of matters that may also be required to be discussed in the financial statement notes.

Firms may also wish to consider the use of a checklist approach to complying with pertinent legal requirements. A checklist that is largely duplicative of the applicable rules, regulations or forms may be no more effective than simply reviewing those rules, regulations or forms, although the checklist could bring diverse requirements together in one document. Perhaps of greater usefulness is a checklist that focuses on less obvious problems that might otherwise be overlooked, in particularly sensitive areas of disclosure, and on the primary sources that should be consulted. An example of such a checklist, prepared for possible use by a firm whose securities practice was restricted almost exclusively to Rule 146 limited partnership syndications, is attached as Appendix C.

D. Backup Reviews

The entire disclosure document should, of course, be reviewed by the partner(s) in charge of a particular transaction. Additional protection against error, and additional evidence of care, results from further review by a partner not primarily responsible for the transaction. This is referred to on occasion as a "cold review," and has been included among procedures adopted in connection with SEC settlements.[134]

However, a true "cold review" is subject to serious limitations. The primary limitation is that an attorney performing a cold review will not have sufficient experience with and information about the client to reliably identify misstatements and omissions. To the extent that the review is conducted by an attorney having additional experience and information, it is no longer a true cold review.

Another limitation is that many transactions involve severe time restrictions, and the insertion of another level of review at the end of the transaction could be a serious problem. If time does not permit this cold review and it was either initially determined that such a review should be

133. This is the letter from the issuer's independent certified public accountants, with respect to financial and other data appearing in a prospectus or other disclosure document, that is typically required by underwriters as a condition of closing a securities offering.

134. See the discussion of the National Student Marketing settlement in Section IV, supra.

made, or there is a general policy of making them, the failure to undertake the cold review would be a breach of internal guidelines that could be asserted as evidence of negligence or recklessness.

Another type of back-up review is to establish a policy of consistently focusing on and resolving disputes or uncertainties over disclosure items. In most instances the disclosure items that could become the focus of a lawsuit receive a higher than normal degree of attention during the preparation of the disclosure document. Either the attorneys or the attorneys and the client together will often have spent considerable time discussing the issue of disclosure and the language to be used for such items. Because there is a nebulous yet real degree of pressure to "get the transaction completed," the use of an attorney not specifically assigned to the transaction to help resolve difficult questions could provide a degree of added objectivity that could prevent some errors. This attorney could regularly participate in the process of resolving disagreements among the attorneys assigned to the transaction or between the attorneys and the client, but would not necessarily be assigned to an overall review at the end of the process. Having participated in these discussions, that attorney would not be in a position to undertake a true cold review, although with the perspective already gained on principal disclosure problems he may serve more effectively in a back-up role than would another attorney.

If the choice is between a "cold review" and the ongoing independent review of uncertainties, it is suggested that the ongoing review has greater potential to yield benefits and does not suffer from the time problems created by a mass of work at the very end of the process.

E. Preparation and Preservation of a Written Record

The engagement letter and schedule of work should define the scope of the representation. However, only a continuous written record and preservation of that record will ensure that, if a dispute later arises, there will be documentation that the roles and functions outlined in the engagement letter and schedule were carried out. In addition, the written record can demonstrate the absence of any recklessness or willfulness, or can provide the basis for a due care defense. While there is always a risk that written materials will contain information that can be used adversely in unexpected circumstances, the authors believe that the ability to demonstrate a careful and conscientious approach to the disclosure process, and to reconstruct the process by which a particular disclosure was shaped, significantly outweigh these risks. Further, the very process of constructing a written record can normally be expected to sharpen an attorney's attention to the disclosure process and thus reduce the likelihood of errors.

An important element of the written record is the preservation of all drafts of the disclosure document that evidence work by various attorneys, or establish that particular disclosures were reviewed by particular officers or others involved in verifying the information. The drafts should be marked so that the attorney involved can be identified, and a record of who is the source of particular information can be conveniently compiled by notations on the drafts at the time the information is added. Correspondence with the client, underwriters, accountants, and other participants should of course be retained, and should be specifically drafted to reflect such important matters as respective duties on particular points, or reliance on a particular party's expertise or representations. Attention should also be paid to the preparation of memoranda concerning disclosure items over which there is any extended discussion, especially where the decision is against disclosure. At a minimum, the rationale for the final decision should be set forth in writing and, when dealing with especially sensitive points, it may also be useful to preserve the specific viewpoints of different attorneys, the client, or any other person contributing to the discussion.

Careful consideration should be given to forming a policy regarding internal drafts of correspondence, memoranda, and other documents. If every draft is retained, attorneys may be inhibited by the process, and may spend unnecessary time making the entire written record read like testimony at a trial. On the other hand, selective discarding of such drafts may make for some unpleasant inferences about why the drafts of a particular document were destroyed. Another alternative, which perhaps avoids these defects, would be a general policy of discarding such drafts, since drafts sent to clients presumably set forth the information intended to be conveyed, coupled with selective retention of drafts that themselves record relevant information about the disclosure process, for example by showing the input of a particular partner.

With respect to any portion of the factual investigation conducted by the law firm, the responsible attorney should be required to provide written back-up material for the facts presented and the process used in determining those facts. In each case in which the law firm is not responsible for undertaking the investigation, the source of the information should be recorded, whether through correspondence, copies of the documents by which the information was obtained (such as the director and officer questionnaires), or even notations in drafts of the disclosure documents. The law firm should normally request and retain schedules to back up summary information provided by the client or other persons; this serves to heighten the source's attention to the process, and also establishes that the attorney was mindful of the possibility that the source could misconstrue exactly what information was sought or could summarize on the basis of assumptions that had not occurred to the attorney.

The written back-up for factual information should ideally be organized as exhibits to an annotated version of the disclosure document. This method makes the material more usable, and makes it more likely that all major points will be covered. However, information that is generated can also be effectively preserved through as simple a means as a single file folder.

Time expended in the transaction should be accurately recorded.   It should be possible to make a reasonable estimate from the time records of the total amount of time expended by attorneys, paralegals, and others in connection with each aspect of the representation.   This information is not only valuable for explaining bills to the clients, but can also be useful in demonstrating that the law firm exercised due diligence and did not act recklessly or willfully.

F. Loose Signature Pages

Registration statements under the 1933 Act are required to be signed by certain officers of the issuer and at least a majority of its directors. In order to deal expediently with the logistical problems of meeting filing deadlines and assembling filing packages in the early morning hours, attorneys frequently ask the signatories to execute signature pages that are not yet bound in with the document to which they will apply.   While this practice is widespread and as a practical matter often necessary, it should be recognized as entailing some liability exposure.   In the event a material misstatement or omission occurred after the signatory last reviewed the registration statement or amendment, he or she could encounter difficulties in establishing a due diligence defense to Section 11 liability; in effect, the signatories are relying completely upon the attorney and the other officers or directors who will be on the scene. Because of this, it appears possible that they may become clients of the attorney under an implied contract theory, and could seek recourse against the attorney.

If this practice is utilized, the signatories should be provided as final a version of the document as possible, preferably in a form that highlights all changes from the previous draft they reviewed.   Where further substantive changes must be made, they should be set forth in writing in as great a detail as the situation permits.   While signatories can still complain that the actual amendment was not precisely the same as the written explanation, that is a better situation than a dispute over its entire content.   Substantive changes that are approved orally should be kept to a minimum, but may be required by the nature of particular transactions.

Section X

SELECTION AND TRAINING OF ATTORNEYS

As should be obvious from the foregoing discussions, the practice of securities law inevitably involves numerous judgments, often under difficult pressures of time and client relations.   It also involves a rapidly changing body of law that can impinge on a transaction from many different directions.   There is no methodology that will prevent all errors in securities transactions, as opposed to reducing the risk that they occur.

Thus, the qualifications of the particular attorneys have a heavy bearing on whether a transaction will be conducted in a manner that will withstand subsequent scrutiny. A firm that is conscientious about reducing the risks of error will carefully consider the background, academic qualifications, temperament and continuing efforts to remain current in the law of the attorneys to whom it entrusts responsibility for securities work.

In addition, the firm should actively encourage continuing legal education in the securities area. This might take the form of required attendance at a minimum of one major program per year, with reports being submitted to other corporate and securities attorneys who did not attend. This type of procedure not only assures that attorneys will have continuing direct exposure to developments in the field, but also that they will approach these sessions with sufficient seriousness to inform their peers. It also provides an occasion for discussion sessions that will permit cross-fertilization of experience and reading, and for continually evaluating the qualifications of particular securities attorneys.

The program for continuing legal education should also include adequate library resources and circulation on a regular basis of current reporting materials. It is also suggested that attorneys working in one particular area of securities law, such as limited partnership private placements, should seek to remain familiar with disclosure and exemption developments in broader areas of securities practice. Otherwise, pertinent developments in such broad concepts as integration, standards of disclosure for insider transactions, and standards for liability, may be overlooked. This suggests that the library of even a firm having a fairly restricted securities practice should contain some treatises and other sources that approach the securities laws from a broader perspective.

The authors believe that a program for selecting, training and maintaining the professional qualifications of securities lawyers will result in reduced risk of errors in securities transactions. Moreover, because of the importance of the individual attorney and his or her qualifications to the conduct of securities transactions, it is suggested that a conscientious program of this nature would also serve as helpful evidence that the firm has not approached a transaction in a willful, reckless or negligent manner.[135]

As part of a program of selecting and training securities attorneys, firms should be conscious not only of the transactions their attorneys are capable of handling, but also of their limitations. It would be unusual, except in a firm having an extensive and specialized securities practice, for a firm to not be confronted from time to time with matters or issues beyond its expertise, or simply as to which more specialized insight would be helpful. For this reason, it is suggested that many firms should

---

135. Rule 2(e) proceedings which have resulted in undertakings with respect to continuing legal education include *In re* John P. O'Neill, SEC Securities Act Release No. 5938 (Aug. 3, 1978), and *In re* Morton Schimmel, SEC Securities Exchange Act Release No. 12254 (March 25, 1976). *See also* the settlement in National Student Marketing Corp., discussed in Section IV, *supra*.

develop a relationship, formal or otherwise, with more specialized counsel who could be conveniently called upon in the event assistance was needed. Obviously, the circumstances for seeking such assistance could vary widely, depending on the firm's level of expertise and specialization, and the nature of the assistance could similarly vary from telephone discussions of particular points to active assistance in the preparation of documents. Interestingly, a requirement that an attorney obtain specialized assistance has been included as a settlement term in several Rule 2(e) proceedings.[136]

136. *See In re* Mary Jane Melrose, SEC Securities Exchange Act Release No. 14720 (May 1, 1978), and *In re* Plotkin, Yolles, Siegel & Turner, SEC Securities Act Release Nos. 5841 (July 5, 1977) and 6105 (Aug. 15, 1979).

APPENDIX A

Dear ———:

As we begin preparing for your proposed offering of securities, we think it important that we set forth the nature of the respective roles that we as counsel and the Company and its personnel will play in the offering. Our objective is to assure that our respective roles are clear, and to help this rather complex process proceed smoothly.

Our primary role is to advise the Company concerning the legal requirements for the transactions that you contemplate, and to provide assistance in preparing the various documents and in obtaining various regulatory approvals. Obviously, our ability to perform these functions effectively depends on our being provided adequate factual information. In this regard, and based on our experience in these matters and on the specific state and federal disclosure requirements, we will from time to time request that specific information be included in the disclosure documents, or that it be provided to us for our consideration. Further, we will review the disclosure documents in a critical frame of mind, with a particular eye to possible inconsistencies or overstated or incomplete information. Also, we will consider the disclosures in the light of significant documents, such as corporate minute books, stock records and important corporate agreements, made available to us. However, we do not have either long-term or intimate familiarity with the Company, and thus will look to you and other corporate personnel to advise us of other information that may be material to an investor's decision. Further, we do not serve as "factual auditors" of the disclosure documents, and the ultimate responsibility for their accuracy and completeness lies with the Company and its personnel.

For these reasons, it is important that you and other senior corporate personnel carefully consider the disclosure documents, constantly questioning not only the accuracy of statements that are made, but also whether there is any undisclosed information that would cause those statements to be viewed in a different light. The main concern is with misstatements or omissions that are "material." For these purposes, information is "material" if there is a substantial likelihood that it would be considered important in the investment decision by a reasonable investor—note that the test turns on whether the investor would consider the information important, not on whether it would cause the investor to make a different decision. Because the concept of materiality is so broad and uncertain, in the case of doubt any question you have should be raised for discussion with us.

Based on our meetings with you, and on my initial review of various documents that you have provided, we are confident that we will not have a difference of opinion as to the legality of proceeding with the offering on the basis of particular disclosures or practices. However, it is important to understand that in the unlikely event of such a difference of opinion we could be obligated, both as a matter of professional standards and protection of ourselves against securities law liability, to withdraw from the representation. We would also be required to take appropriate steps to assure that other parties who might be relying on our participation as counsel were aware of our withdrawal. In addition, the Company would remain obligated to compensate us for the time we had devoted to the matter to the date of withdrawal, at our normal hourly rates.

We understand that we are acting as securities counsel to the Company in this transaction, and that we are not acting as its general corporate attorneys. While we will be reviewing basic corporate documentation, and making certain suggestions for by-law amendments and ratifying resolutions, we will be relying on the Company's regular corporate counsel for assurance that corporate actions are taken in conformity with governing documents and state statutes, and generally with respect to questions of state corporate law.

As we have discussed, we will be billing for our services at our standard rates, which range from $X per hour for senior partner time and $Y for mine, to $Z an hour for the time of a first-year associate. In addition, upon successful completion of the exemptive and registration procedures, we will consider a modest premium, probably in the neighborhood of A–B%, to reflect the inherent risks to us of acting as counsel in securities transactions, and of rendering our opinion in connection with them. In considering any premium, we will take into account the efficiency with which we have provided our services. As we have also discussed, we would expect that the total bill for our services, through the point at which the offering may commence, would not exceed $C, including any premium. However, the total amount of time that we must devote will depend on such matters as the extent of delays and difficulties encountered in the administrative review process, the nature of any legal problems and issues that may arise, and the ease with which you and the Indenture Trustee agree on the terms and form of the Indenture. Obviously, the amount of work required will be greater, and will be more difficult to determine in advance, during the Company's initial offering than in subsequent offerings when we will be traveling a previously-charted path.

We will bill the Company on a monthly basis. As agreed, payment will be made promptly unless you have a question concerning the bill. If so, you have agreed to bring such matters to our attention immediately.

If you have any questions about this letter, or if you have other thoughts as to the appropriate relationship between the Company and our firm, we should discuss the situation further. In addition, if at any time you are concerned in any way with the nature of our services or the manner in which we are providing them, we urge you to raise the matter with us. This is an important aspect of any professional relationship, and we approach it openly and without defensiveness.

We are very pleased to have the opportunity to work with you in this initial offering, and are hopeful that we will be developing a long-term and highly enjoyable relationship with you and the Company.

Very truly yours,

APPENDIX B

QUESTIONNAIRE FOR OFFICERS AND DIRECTORS OF ———— CORP.

Please complete and return this questionnaire to ———— no later than ————, 1979.

This questionnaire is being directed to the officers and directors of the Company to obtain information to be used in connection with the preparation of documents that will be filed with the Securities and Exchange Commission, including the Annual Report on Form 10–K, proxy materials and a registration statement for an offering of Common Shares.

If additional space is needed for a complete answer, please use the back of this form or attach a separate sheet, and make appropriate cross-references.

Unless otherwise indicated, please answer all questions, using "None" or "Not Applicable" where appropriate.

1. *Security Holdings*

(a) State separately as of the most recent practicable date the number of Common Shares of the Company registered in the name of:

Number of Shares

(1) You.

(2) Any trust or estate of which you are a beneficiary.

(3) Any trust of which you are a settlor if you have the power to revoke the trust without obtain–ing consent of all the beneficiaries.

(4) Any partnership or investment club in which you have an interest.

(5) Any other person (*including your spouse or children*), trust, brokerage firm, nominee, partnership or corporation, *if* as to such security you have *or* share

"voting power" or "investment power."*

* "Voting power" includes the power to vote, or direct the voting of, the
security; "investment power" includes the power to dispose, or to direct
the disposition, of the security.

NOTE: If there are Common Shares registered in any other way in
which you think you may have a beneficial interest, please so note in the
space below so that the question may be pursued.

You may disclaim all beneficial interest in any of the securities listed in
your response to this question. If you wish to disclaim such beneficial
interest, please identify the securities involved and the record owners
thereof.

(b) Do you or any of the persons listed above have any right to
acquire Shares, whether through exercise of options, warrants or similar
rights, through revocation of a trust, discretionary account or similar
arrangement, or otherwise? YES ——— NO ———.

If "Yes," please explain.

2. *Options*

(a) Do you hold any options to purchase securities of the Company?
YES ——— NO ———.

If "Yes," please state the class and amount of securities subject to, and
expiration date(s) of, your options, and the option price(s).

(b) During the fiscal year ended ———, 1979, were you granted any
options to acquire Company securities? YES ——— NO ———.

If "Yes," please state the class and amount of securities subject to, and
expiration date(s) of, your options, and the option price(s).

(c) During the fiscal year, have you exercised any such options? YES
——— NO ———.

If "Yes," please explain.

3. *Remuneration*

(a) Please state the amount of all cash remuneration distributed to you or accrued for you by the Company during the fiscal year ended ———, 1979. Please include all salary, professional fees, directors' fees, commissions and bonuses. (Remuneration paid to a partnership in which you were a partner is not to be included, but should be indicated in the answer to Question 4(b)).

(b) During the fiscal year ended ———, 1979, have you acquired or been given the right to acquire securities or property from the Company at below their market value (you need not include share options reported in response to Question 2(b))? YES ——— NO ———.

If "Yes," please explain.

(c) Does the Company pay the premium for any life or health insurance policies insuring you, or provide you any benefit under medical reimbursement plans, under plans or programs that are not available on a comparable basis to substantially all Company employees? YES ——— NO ———.

If "Yes," please identify the plan.

(d) During the fiscal year ended ———, 1979, did you receive any other personal benefits provided by the Company which are not directly related to your job performance and are not available to substantially all Company employees on a similar basis (examples of such personal benefits could be personal use of Company automobiles or other property, personal legal, accounting or other services provided at the Company's expense, and repairs or maintenance of personal property performed by or at the Company's expense)? YES ——— NO ———.

If "Yes," please explain.

(e) Identify any pension or retirement plans, annuity contracts, deferred compensation plans, stock purchase plans, incentive compensation plans, thrift plans or similar plans under which you were covered or were a participant during the fiscal year ended ———, 1979, other than the stock bonus plan, the stock option plan, and the retirement plan.

(f) Describe below all remuneration proposed to be paid to you in the future, directly or indirectly, by the Company pursuant to any existing plan or arrangement other than as described in Questions 3(a), (b), (c), (d) and (e). State both estimated future benefits and amounts actually set aside or accrued during the fiscal year ended ———, 1979.

(g) During the fiscal year ended ———, 1979, did you receive any cash remuneration, or any non-cash benefits of the types described in Questions 3(b), (c), (d) and (e), from any party other than the Company, pursuant to a transaction between the Company and that other party the primary purpose of which was to provide you such remuneration or benefits? YES ——— NO ———.

Are any such remuneration or benefits proposed to be paid to you in future pursuant to any such transactions? YES ——— NO ———.

If "Yes" to either question, please explain.

4. *Interest in Any Transaction.* (If you have any doubt as to the application of the questions under this heading, please communicate with ——— at ———.

This series of questions deals with your interest, direct or indirect, in any transactions to which the Company was or may be a party. Please describe any such transactions fully and state the amount or approximate amount of your interest and that of any other person or organization addressed by the question. No information need be furnished with respect to a loan transaction where the indebtedness does not exceed $10,000 or for other transactions where the total amount involved (including the total of all periodic or installment payments) does not exceed $40,000; a series of related transactions should be treated as one transaction for these purposes. You also need not furnish information with respect to transactions included in your responses to Questions 2 or 3, or with respect to transactions (such as the receipt of dividends or interest) arising solely from your status as a holder of, and in common with other holders of, the Company's securities.

(a) Describe any contract (rental or otherwise), loan agreement, debtor/creditor relationship, or other transaction which you have had or which has been in effect between you and the Company or any of its subsidiaries during the past three years. Information concerning transactions should include the principal or consideration received or paid by you and the consideration paid or received by the Company.

(b) Answer Question 4(a) as it would apply, not to you, but to any corporation or organization (other than the Company) of which you are, or at the time of the transaction were, (i) an officer, (ii) a partner, (iii) directly or indirectly the beneficial owner of 10% or more of any class of its equity securities, or (iv) together with other directors and officers of the Company, the beneficial owners, in the aggregate, of 10% or more of any class of its equity securities.

(c) Answer Question 4(a) as it would apply to any trust or estate of which a beneficiary is you, your wife, any of your minor children, or any relative of you or your wife who lives in your household or who is a director or officer of the Company or any of its subsidiaries, or of which you are a trustee.

(d) Answer Question 4(a) as it would apply to your wife or any other relative of yours or of your wife (including your children) who lives in your home or who is a director or officer of the Company or any of its subsidiaries, and indicate your relationship to the person or persons involved in the transaction.

(e) Answer Questions 4(a) through 4(d) as they would apply to any presently proposed transactions.

5. *Legal Proceedings*

(a) Are you, or any of the persons described in Questions 4(b)-(d), a party adverse to the Company in any pending legal proceeding to which the Company is a party or of which any Company property is the subject? YES ——— NO ———.

If "Yes," please give details, including the name of the court or agency in which such proceeding is pending, the date it was instituted, the principal parties thereto, and the nature of your adverse interest.

(b) Do you know of any pending legal proceedings in which the party adverse to the Company is the record or beneficial holder of 5% of the

Company's Common Shares, or is related to or associated with such a security holder? YES ——— NO ———.

If "Yes," please explain.

6. *Conflicting Activities.* Have you, or any of the persons described in Questions 4(b)-(d), engaged in, or are you or any such persons now engaged in, any activities which conflict with the Company's business operations or objectives? YES ——— NO ———.

If "Yes," please describe, identifying the nature of the activities and your, or such persons' participation in them.

7. *Indemnification.* Do you know of any contract or arrangement under which any director or officer of the Company is insured or indemnified in any manner against any liability which he may incur as a trustee or officer? YES ——— NO ———.

If "Yes," please identify and state the general effect of any such contract or arrangement.

8. *5% Security Holders*

(a) Do you know of any person who owns beneficially more than 5% of the Company's outstanding Shares? YES ——— NO ———.

If "Yes,"please identify such person or group and, if known, the amounts so owned.

(b) Answer Question (a) as it would apply to any partnership, syndicate or other group of two or more persons acting together for the purpose of acquiring, holding or disposing of such securities. YES ——— NO ———.

(c) Do you know of any voting trust or similar agreement under which more than 5% of the Company's outstanding Shares is or is to be held? YES ——— NO ———.

If "Yes," please give details about such trust or agreement.

9. *Independent Certified Public Accountants.* Are you, or have you at any time been, interested in or affiliated or connected with ———, independent certified public accountants? YES ——— NO ———.

If "Yes," please state the nature of any such interest, connection or affiliation.

———————

If you are a director or executive officer, please complete Questions 10–14. Otherwise, you may skip those questions and proceed directly to the signature page. The term "executive officer" means the President, Secretary, Treasurer, any Vice President in charge of a principal business function, and any other officer who performs similar policy-making functions for the Company.

10. *Positions Held and Employment History.* State the name and nature of all positions and offices that you hold, or are to hold, with the Company. If you are an officer, please state the date you were appointed to the office you now hold, and if you are a director, the date on which your present term will expire. Describe all principal occupations and employments during the past five years. Please include the name and the principal business of each corporation or organization with which such occupations or employments were carried on.

NOTE: Persons listed on the sheet attached to their copies of this questionnaire may comply with this request by initialing same and making appropriate changes, if any, to the data appearing thereon [attachment omitted].

11. Are there any arrangements or understandings (other than with respect to duties and terms of employment reflected in previous responses) between you and any other persons pursuant to which you have been selected as a director or officer? YES ——— NO ———.

If "Yes," please explain.

12. If you are a director, do you hold any directorships in any other company having a class of securities registered with the SEC under the 1934 Act, or which is registered with the SEC as an investment company? YES ——— NO ———.

If "Yes," please state the name of such company, the date on which you became a director, and the date on which your present term expires.

13. Please give your date of birth and state the nature of any family relationships between yourself and any other director or executive officer of the Company.

NOTE: The term "family relationship" means any relationship, by blood, marriage or adoption, not more remote than first cousin.

14. During the past five years:

(a) Have you filed, or has there been filed against you, a petition under the Bankruptcy Act or any state insolvency law (YES ——— NO ———), or has a receiver, fiscal agent or similar officer been appointed by a court for any business or property of yours (YES ——— NO ———), of any partnership in which you were a general partner at or within two years before the time of such filing (YES ——— NO ———), or of any corporation or business association of which you were an executive officer at or within two years before the time of such filing (YES ——— NO ———)?

(b) Have you been convicted in a criminal proceeding (excluding traffic violations and other minor offences) (YES ——— NO ———), or are you the subject of a criminal proceeding which is presently pending (YES ——— NO ———)?

(c) Have you been the subject of any order, judgment or decree of any court of competent jurisdiction permanently or temporarily enjoining you from acting as, or limiting your activities as, an investment adviser, underwriter, broker or dealer in securities (YES ——— NO ———), or as an affiliated person (see the NOTE below), director or employee of any investment company, bank, savings and loan association or insurance company (YES ——— NO ———), or from engaging in or continuing any conduct or practice in connection with any such activity, or from engaging in any type of business practice (YES ——— NO ———), or have you been the subject of any order of a federal or state authority barring, suspending, or otherwise limiting for more than 60 days your right to be engaged in any such activity or to be associated with persons engaged in such activity (YES ——— NO ———)?

If the answer to any of the foregoing questions is "Yes," please explain below.

NOTE: You may be deemed to be an "affiliate" of a person if you control that person, either directly or indirectly through one or more intermediaries. You may be deemed to control a person if you are an officer or director of that person or if you own beneficially 10% or more of its equity securities or if you otherwise control such person. You will be deemed to control a person if you possess the power to direct or cause the direction of the management and policies of the person.

*   *   *

The above information is supplied by me at the request of the Company for use in connection with formal documents to be filed with the Securities and Exchange Commission, including the Company's Annual Report on Form 10-K, proxy materials and a registration statement for an offering of Common Shares. I understand that the information will be relied upon by the Company, by its counsel, and by other parties participating in the filing of such documents. To the best of my knowledge, information and belief, the information is correctly stated. I agree immediately to notify ———— of any changes in the foregoing information that should be made as a result of any purchase or sale of securities or other developments.

SIGNATURE:

PRINTED NAME:

DATE:

APPENDIX C

RULE 146   PRIVATE PLACEMENTS

Checklist

Note : This checklist is *not* a guide to the proper structuring and execution of Rule 146 private placements. It is not a substitute for careful reading of the applicable rules and regulations, and is not intended as a securities law reference source. It intentionally omits reference to several of the obvious requirements of Rule 146, such as number of purchasers, sales methods, and filing of Form 146. It is designed solely to highlight particular critical areas for disclosure and inquiry, and to assure that counsel has focused on questions and matters that might otherwise be overlooked and thus be a potential basis for liability of the client or counsel.

* * *

1.   What are the parameters of the offering?—the integration doctrine (see SEC Release No. 33–4552 (November 6, 1962)).

Has the same entity issued similar securities within the past year? Yes ___ No ___

Has the same entity issued any other securities within the past six months?   Yes ___ No ___

Have similar or any other securities been issued within the foregoing time periods by any entity affiliated with the issuer (e.g., parents, subsidiaries or sister entities)?   Yes ___ No ___

Have securities been issued by entities, otherwise unrelated, that have been sponsored, promoted or otherwise controlled by the same person or persons filling any such role with respect to the issuer? Yes ___ No ___

If any of the foregoing questions has been answered "Yes," careful consideration should be given to the effects of the integration doctrine.

2.   Who are the promoters?

It should be noted that the applicable definition appears in Rule 251 of Regulation A, or Rule 405(q) of Regulation C, depending on which disclosure guide is applicable (see Item 3 below). It should also be noted that these definitions (which are identical) are broadly written. Serious consideration should be given to the status as a promoter of any individual who is a moving force in a transaction involving the organization of a tax shelter entity. Reality rather than technicality should be the guide in approaching this question.

3. What is the applicable guide to adequate disclosure under Rule 146(e), the applicable registration form (e.g., Form S–1), for offerings in excess of $1,500,000, or Schedule I of Regulation A, for offerings not exceeding $1,500,000?

Has the applicable disclosure guide been checked on a point-by-point basis against the disclosures contained in the offering circular? Has this review, when keyed to a registration form, included consideration of Regulation S–K and the Guides to Preparation of Registration Statements? Yes ___ No ___

Note that compliance with the disclosure requirements is a condition of the exemption; thus, inadequate disclosure involves exposure to both fraud and non-registration causes of action.

4. To assure compliance with the requirements of Item 9 of Schedule I, or of Items 3, 4 and 6 of Regulation S–K, have all general partners, promoters, directors, officers or other principals been questioned with respect to the matters discussed in those provisions, and have they completed and signed an appropriate questionnaire? Yes ___ No ___

This is another area in which the applicable disclosure provisions are broadly worded, and in which reality should supplant technicality. Specific inquiries should be directed at such possible insider relationships and benefits as fees arising from the distribution process and from insurance, brokerage or advisory activities. Consideration should also be given to future services, sales or leases of property and such indirect benefits as more favorable treatment than that obtained by the issuer from a third-party vendor with whom the issuer will be doing business. Even if Schedule I is the applicable disclosure guide, reference to Item 4 of Regulation S–K may be useful in evaluating the types of relationships that may be deemed material.

5. Has consideration been given to any conflict of interests that counsel may have that may be material to an evaluation by investors of counsel's legal opinions or other representations? Yes ___ No ___

Attention should be directed to whether payment of fees is, either by agreement or as a matter of circumstance, contingent upon the closing of the transaction; to any finders' fees or other distribution-related fees payable to counsel; and to counsel's on-going relationship with the issuer or its principals or promoters. The materiality of such information would be affected not only by the size of payments involved, but also by the nature of counsel's opinions and representations. Such information may be viewed as considerably more material in instances where the legal judgments involved are difficult and uncertain, and where the investors are likely to be relying heavily upon counsel.

6. Does the offering circular contain a clear and concise description of the method of distribution, and an appropriate underwriting discount table? Yes ___ No ___

This information is specifically required by paragraphs 3, 4 and 5 of Schedule I and Items 1 and 2 of Form S–1.

7. Have discussions of the nature and outlook of the business venture been tested and supported? In particular:

Is there written documentation for the various assertions and representations? Yes ＿ No ＿

Is there contrary information that has not been disclosed, or undisclosed information from which contrary inferences may be drawn? Yes ＿ No ＿

Is there a discussion of the background of persons expressing opinions or beliefs, including information (such as prior erroneous opinions and beliefs) that would be material to evaluating the particular opinion or belief? Yes ＿ No ＿

With respect to information included on the authority of an "independent" party, is there any undisclosed information casting doubt on the party's independence? (Consideration should be given to the amount of compensation, the extent of similar services controlled by the issuer's promoters or other principals, the difficulty experienced in finding the independent party, and whether persons having greater experience or expertise have either declined to act in the matter or have not been approached because of an expectation that they would decline). Yes ＿ No ＿

8. Has consideration been given to compliance by all persons involved in the selling process (including those receiving finders' fees) with the applicable broker-dealer laws? Yes ＿ No ＿

INDEX

INDEX

†